Get set for the Maths SATS with CGP!

This fantastic CGP book is fully up-to-date
for the new KS2 Maths SATS in 2016 and beyond!

It explains all the key Maths topics from Years 5 and 6
with crystal-clear notes and helpful step-by-step examples.

There are even practice questions to test them on what
they've learned — with answers included at the back!

What CGP is all about

Our sole aim here at CGP is to produce the highest quality books
— carefully written, immaculately presented and
dangerously close to being funny.

Then we work our socks off to get them out to you
— at the cheapest possible prices.

Contents

Published by CGP

Editors:
Joanna Daniels, Ceara Hayden, Sharon Keeley-Holden, Kirstie McHale, Caley Simpson

ISBN: 978 1 78294 419 5

With thanks to Alison Palin and Maxine Petrie for the proofreading.
Also thanks to Laura Jakubowski for the copyright research.

Thumb illustration used throughout the book © iStockphoto.com.

Contains public sector information licensed under the Open Government Licence v3.0.
http://www.nationalarchives.gov.uk/doc/open-government-licence/version/3/

Printed by Elanders Ltd, Newcastle upon Tyne.
Clipart from Corel®

Based on the classic CGP style created by Richard Parsons.

About This Book

This Book has All the Key Topics for KS2

At the end of Year 6, you'll be tested on all the maths you've learnt during Key Stage 2. This book covers the key topics you might be tested on.

This book covers the key Learning Objectives for Years 5-6 of the National Curriculum.

There are two pages on each topic
One page explains the maths.
The other page has worked examples.
These show you how to answer questions.

There are Practice Questions for Each Section

At the end of each section there are practice questions.
You can see what you know and what you don't know.

There's a matching Question Book.
It's got questions on all the topics and it also has some practice tests.

I love to practise.
I love to practise.

There are Learning Objectives on All Topics

Learning objectives say what you should be able to do.
Use the tick circles to show how confident you feel.

Tick here if you think you need a bit more practice.

If you're really struggling, tick here.

Tick this circle if you can do all the maths on the page.

"I can multiply a four-digit number by a two-digit number."

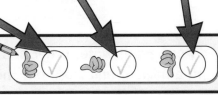

Ordering Numbers

7-digit Numbers are into the Millions

Look at this whopping number — the digit furthest to the left is the millions:

hundred thousands

thousands

tens

6 548 372

millions

ten thousands

hundreds

units

With big numbers, put a space after every 3 digits, starting from the units.

So, it's:

"Six million, five hundred and forty eight thousand, three hundred and seventy two."

You can partition it into:
6 000 000 + 500 000 + 40 000 + 8000 + 300 + 70 + 2

EXAMPLE:

James caught one hundred and three thousand, eight hundred and twenty four fish.
Write this out as a number.

103 824 fish

one hundred and three thousand   eight hundred and twenty four

Big Numbers Can Be Ordered

EXAMPLE: Put these numbers in descending order:
5321, 66 354, 6852, 5789

Descending means going from largest to smallest.

66 354   6852   5321   5789

This is the largest. It's the only one with ten thousands.

This is the next largest. It has more thousands than 5321 or 5789.

Now compare 5321 and 5789. They both have 5 thousands. So look at the hundreds. 5789 is larger than 5321.

So the right order is: 66 354, 6852, 5789, 5321.

"I can read, write, order and compare numbers up to a million, and work out the value of each digit."

Worked Examples

① Roonie's website gets **4 352 801** hits each year.
What are the values of **4** and **2** in this number?

4 millions  four million

2 thousands two thousand

1) Look at where <u>4</u> is in the number and write the digit in <u>words</u>.

2) Now look at where <u>2</u> is in the number and write the digit in <u>words</u>.

② Downton Zoo had **nine hundred and twenty six thousand, eight hundred and sixty three** visitors last year. Write this amount as a **number**.

1) Write down the number of <u>thousands</u>.

2) Then write down the number of <u>hundreds</u>, <u>tens</u> and <u>units</u>.

3) Now write the <u>number</u> completely.

926 thousand

863

 926 863 visitors

③ Martin has three rabbits. They weigh **2564 g**, **2587 g** and **2751 g**.
Arrange these weights in **ascending** order.

1) Compare the digits in the <u>thousands</u> column first.

2) All the numbers have <u>2 thousands</u>, so next compare the digits in the <u>hundreds</u> column. **2751** is the <u>largest</u> as it has the <u>most hundreds</u>.

3) Compare the digits in the <u>tens</u> column. You can use the < or > signs to show which number is <u>larger</u>.

4) Now <u>arrange</u> the weights from smallest to largest (that's what <u>ascending order</u> means).

2<u>5</u>64 has a <u>5</u> in the hundreds column
2<u>5</u>87 has a <u>5</u> in the hundreds column
2<u>7</u>51 has a <u>7</u> in this column, so is larger

25<u>6</u>4 has a <u>6</u> in the tens column
25<u>8</u>7 has a <u>8</u> in this column, so is larger

2564 < 2587 — < means 'is less than' and > means 'is greater than'.

 2564 g, 2587 g, 2751 g

Numbers are always being told to line up...

When you're asked to order numbers by their size, don't forget that 'ascending' means from smallest to largest and 'descending' means from largest to smallest.

Negative Numbers

Adding and Subtracting Negative Numbers

Number lines are really useful for problems using <u>negative numbers</u>.

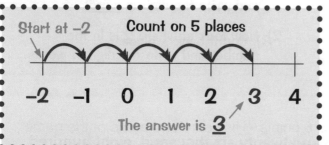

EXAMPLES: What is –2 + 5?

Start at –2   Count on 5 places

–2 –1 0 1 2 3 4

The answer is **3**

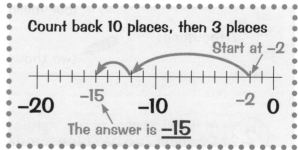

Work out –2 – 13.

Count back 10 places, then 3 places

Start at –2

–20   –15   –10   –2   0

The answer is **–15**

EXAMPLE: The temperature in George's cellar is <u>8 °C</u>. The temperature in his garden is <u>10 °C</u> colder. What is the temperature in his garden?

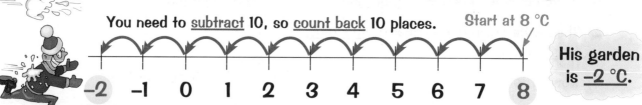

You need to <u>subtract</u> 10, so <u>count back</u> 10 places.   Start at 8 °C

–2 –1 0 1 2 3 4 5 6 7 8

His garden is <u>–2 °C</u>.

Working Out Differences

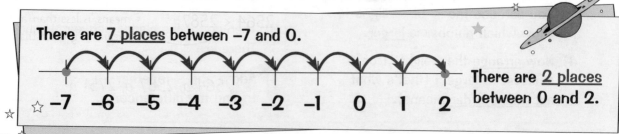

EXAMPLE: The temperature inside a rocket is <u>2 °C</u>.
The temperature outside a rocket is <u>–7 °C</u>.
What is the <u>difference</u> between these temperatures?

Do a quick sketch of the number line. Mark the two temperatures on it, then <u>count how many places</u> there are between them.

It's often easiest to count the places <u>to zero</u>, then the number of places <u>after zero</u> and then add them together.

There are <u>7 places</u> between –7 and 0.

–7 –6 –5 –4 –3 –2 –1 0 1 2

There are <u>2 places</u> between 0 and 2.

So the difference in temperature is 7 + 2 = <u>9 °C</u>.

"I can calculate using negative numbers."

Worked Examples

1 Work out −3 − 5.

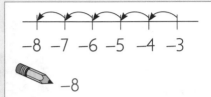

−8 −7 −6 −5 −4 −3

−8

1) Draw a number line first.
2) Start at −3.
3) Count back 5 places.

2 At the start of a game, Matteo has **6** points. His score at the end of the game is **9** points **lower** than the score he started with. What is his final score?

1) Draw a number line first.
2) Start at 6.
3) Then count back 9 places.

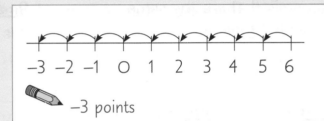

−3 −2 −1 0 1 2 3 4 5 6

−3 points

3 This table shows what is sold on each level of a superstore. Work out the difference in levels between **clothes** and **electronics**.

Items	Level
Toys	5
Clothes	−2
Electronics	6

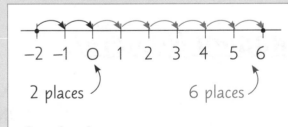

−2 −1 0 1 2 3 4 5 6

2 places   6 places

2 + 6 = 8

8 levels

1) Draw a number line first. Mark the two values on it, and count how many places there are between them.
2) First count the places between −2 and 0. There are 2 places.
3) Then count the places between 0 and 6. There are 6 places.
4) Add 2 and 6 together to find the difference.

These pages make me feel cold...

...but if you work hard enough, you'll soon start to warm up. Make sure you feel comfortable using negative numbers — this isn't the last you'll see of them.

Roman Numerals

The Romans Used Numerals Instead of Digits

The Romans used <u>letters</u> called <u>numerals</u> instead of the <u>digits 0-9</u>.
You need to know these numerals:

> I = 1   X = 10   C = 100   M = 1000
> V = 5   L = 50   D = 500

For <u>other</u> numbers, they put <u>numerals in a row</u>.
Here are the <u>rules</u> you need to read them:

Numerals that are <u>the same</u> are <u>added together</u>. III = 3 XX = 20 CC = 200	<u>Small</u> numerals <u>after</u> big ones are <u>added on</u> to the big one. XII = 12 CI = 101 CCXXX = 230

<u>Small</u> numerals <u>before</u> big ones are <u>subtracted</u> from the big one. (These six are the only subtractions allowed.)	IV = 4 XL = 40 CD = 400 IX = 9 XC = 90 CM = 900

Do any <u>subtracting</u> BEFORE doing any <u>adding</u>.

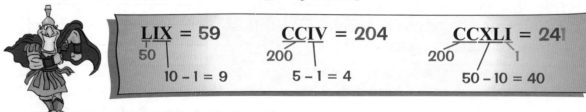

> L<u>IX</u> = 59   <u>CC</u>IV = 204   <u>CC</u>X<u>LI</u> = 241
> 50│   200 │   200   │   1
>   10 − 1 = 9   5 − 1 = 4   50 − 10 = 40

You Can Write Years In Roman Numerals

<u>2000</u> is written <u>MM</u> so years in the 2000s will begin MM   **MMXVI**
2016

<u>1900</u> is written <u>MCM</u> so years in the 1900s will begin MCM   **MCMXXIV**
1924

<u>1800</u> is written <u>MDCCC</u> so years in the 1800s will begin MDCCC   **MDCCCLXXIII**
1873

"I can read Roman numerals up to M and recognise years written in Roman numerals."

Worked Examples

1 What number is shown by the Roman numeral **MDIV**?

1) Write down the value of <u>M</u>.

2) Then write down the value of <u>D</u>.

3) <u>IV</u> has a small numeral <u>before</u> a big one, so you'll need to <u>subtract</u>.

4) Now <u>add</u> them together.

M = 1000

D = 500

IV = 5 − 1 = 4

1000 + 500 + 4 = 1504

2 Write **DCLXXXIX** as a number.

D = 500   C = 100   L = 50

X = 10, so XXX = 30

X = 10 and I = 1, so IX = 10 − 1 = 9

500 + 100 + 50 + 30 + 9
= 689

1) Write down the values of <u>D</u>, <u>C</u> and <u>L</u>.

2) For <u>XXX</u> you need to add (numerals that are <u>the same</u> are <u>added together</u>).

3) <u>IX</u> has a small numeral <u>before</u> a big one, so you'll need to <u>subtract</u>.

4) Now <u>add</u> all of these numbers up.

3 Dilna's great, great, great, great grandfather was born in **MDCCCXIX**. What year is this?

1) Start with any <u>subtracting</u>.

2) You can then <u>add</u> this to <u>X</u>.

3) You know that <u>MDCCC</u> is <u>1800</u>...

4) ...so <u>add</u> this to <u>XIX</u>.

IX = 10 − 1 = 9

X = 10, so XIX = 10 + 9 = 19

MDCCC = 1800

1800 + 19 = 1819

<u>I, II, III, IV, V, once I caught a fish alive...</u>

The Romans had a different way of writing numbers — which can be a bit confusing. Make sure you're happy with how to write Roman numerals as numbers.

Decimals

Decimals — the Basics

Decimals are one way to write numbers that <u>aren't whole numbers</u>.
<u>Whole numbers</u> have units, tens, hundreds and so on.
<u>Decimal numbers</u> also have <u>tenths</u>, <u>hundredths</u> and <u>thousandths</u>...

u	t	h	th	
4 . 0	0	2		is just a bit bigger than 4
4 . 5	0	0		is halfway between 4 and 5
4 . 9	7	6		is just a bit less than 5

You can partition decimals.
$4.976 = 4 + 0.9 + 0.07 + 0.006$

units   tenths   hundredths   thousandths

Decimal Places Come After the Decimal Point

Each digit after the decimal point is called a <u>decimal place</u> (d.p.).
They're numbered starting from <u>1</u>.

So if a number has <u>1</u> decimal place, it has <u>1</u> digit after the decimal point.

u   t   h   th

0.642

1st decimal place
2nd decimal place
3rd decimal place

Ordering Decimals

Here's how you order decimals from smallest to largest.

> To order from largest to smallest do the same, but arrange from largest to smallest at each step.

STEP 1 — Arrange all the numbers in <u>place value columns</u>. (Make sure all the decimal points are <u>underneath</u> each other.)

STEP 2 — Make all the numbers the <u>same length</u> by filling in extra zeros.

STEP 3 — Look at the <u>whole number</u> part of each decimal number. Arrange the numbers from smallest to largest.

STEP 4 — If any whole numbers are the same, look at the digits in the <u>tenths</u> column. Arrange them from smallest to largest.

STEP 5 — If any of the tenths are the same, look at the digits in the <u>hundredths</u> column. Arrange them from smallest to largest.

STEP 6 — If any of the hundredths are the same, look at the digits in the <u>thousandths</u> column. Arrange them from smallest to largest.

"I can identify the value of each digit to three decimal places. I can order and compare numbers with up to three decimal places."

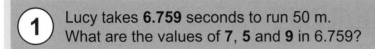

Worked Examples

1 Lucy takes **6.759** seconds to run 50 m.
What are the values of **7**, **5** and **9** in 6.759?

7 tenths Seven tenths

5 hundredths Five hundredths

9 thousandths Nine thousandths

1) Look at where the 7 is and write it out in words.

2) Now look at where the 5 is and write it out in words.

3) Finally, do the same for the 9.

2 How many **hundredths** are there in **6.984**?

The first decimal place gives tenths, the second decimal place gives hundredths and the third decimal place gives thousandths. So look at the second decimal place.

6.9**8**4

 8 hundredths

3 Order these numbers from **largest** to **smallest**: **0.5, 2.03, 0.67, 0.842, 0.895**.

1) Arrange all the numbers in place value columns and make them the same length by filling in extra zeros.

2) Look at the whole number part and arrange from largest to smallest.

3) Four numbers start with 0, so compare their digits in the tenths column. Arrange these from largest to smallest.

4) 0.842 and 0.895 have the same digits in the tenths column. Compare the digits in the hundredths column.

0.500	2.030	2.030	2.030
2.030	0.500	0.842	0.895
0.670	0.670	0.895	0.842
0.842	0.842	0.670	0.670
0.895	0.895	0.500	0.500

 2.03, 0.895, 0.842, 0.67, 0.5

Let's get straight to the point...

Decimals are super important. You need to get used to using them — so go through these worked examples carefully. You'll soon realise that they don't bite.

Rounding Off

Rounding Whole Numbers

This is quite easy if you remember the <u>RULES</u>:

1) The number lies <u>between two possible answers</u>. You have to decide which one it's <u>nearer to</u>.
2) Look at the digit <u>to the right</u> of the place you're rounding to — the DECIDER.
3) If the decider is <u>5 or more</u> then <u>round UP</u>. If the decider is <u>less than 5</u> then <u>round DOWN</u>.

Th	H	T	u
3	7	2	4

For example, if you round to the nearest <u>Hundred</u>, the <u>decider</u> is the <u>Tens</u> digit — here it's 2.

EXAMPLES: Emily has 213 freckles. Round 213 to the <u>nearest hundred</u>.

213 is between 200 and 300.

The decider is 1 so <u>round down</u> to <u>200</u>.

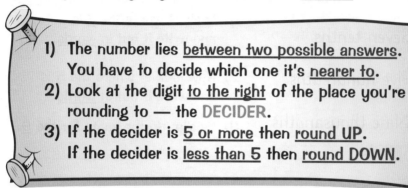

My very rare elephant weighs 68 987 g.
How much does he weigh to the <u>nearest ten thousand grams</u>?

68 987 is between 60 000 and 70 000.
The decider is 8 so <u>round up</u> to <u>70 000</u> g.
(On a number line, you can see it's closer to 70 000 than 60 000.)

60 000   65 000   70 000

Rounding to 1 Decimal Place

This is easy if you stick to the <u>rounding rules</u>. You're rounding to 1 d.p. so look at the digit to the <u>right</u> of that — the <u>second decimal place</u>, to decide whether to round up or down.

This is the decider.

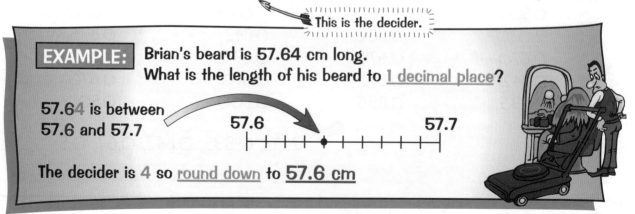

EXAMPLE: Brian's beard is 57.64 cm long.
What is the length of his beard to <u>1 decimal place</u>?

57.64 is between
57.6 and 57.7

57.6   57.7

The decider is 4 so <u>round down</u> to <u>57.6 cm</u>

"I can round any whole number. I can round decimals to one decimal place or the nearest whole number."

Worked Examples

1 Niko sent **2163** text messages last year.
Round this number to the nearest **thousand**.

1) Find the two numbers in the <u>thousands</u> that Niko's number of text messages lies between.

2) Now look at the digit to the <u>right</u> of the thousands (the <u>decider</u>).

3) 1 is <u>less</u> than 5, so <u>round down</u>.

2163 is between
2000 and 3000

2<u>1</u>63

 2000

2 David has just signed a **£7 365 212** deal with a football team.
Round this amount to the nearest **hundred thousand**.

7 365 212 is between
7 300 000 and 7 400 000

7 3<u>6</u>5 212

 £7 400 000

1) Find the two numbers in the <u>hundred thousands</u> that the amount lies between.

2) Now look at the digit to the <u>right</u> of the hundred thousands (the <u>decider</u>).

3) 6 is <u>more</u> than 5, so <u>round up</u>.

3 Philippa buys **6.82 kg** of ice cream and **2.45 kg** of jelly for her party.
Round the amount of ice cream to the nearest **whole number** and the amount of jelly to **1 decimal place**.

1) Start with the amount of ice cream.
Find the two <u>whole numbers</u> that it lies between.

2) You're rounding to a <u>whole number</u>, so look at the digit in the <u>first</u> decimal place (the <u>decider</u>).

3) 8 is <u>more</u> than 5, so <u>round up</u>.

4) Now look at the amount of jelly. Find the two numbers with <u>1 decimal place</u> that it lies between.

5) You're rounding to <u>1 decimal place</u> so look at the digit in the second decimal place (the <u>decider</u>).

6) The decider is 5, so <u>round up</u>.

6.82 is between 6 and 7.

6.<u>8</u>2

 7 kg of ice cream

2.45 is between 2.4 and 2.5.

2.4<u>5</u>

 2.5 kg of jelly

Round and round the garden, like a...

...Maths explorer. Working out which number is the decider is the key to rounding.
So make sure you remember, it's the digit to the right of the place you're rounding to.

Practice Questions

1   Charlie is flying round the world. He has already flown 3 872 651 m.

    a)   What is the value of 6 in this number?

    b)   Write 3 872 651 out in words.

2   Katie wins six hundred thousand, two hundred and eighty one pounds on a quiz show.

    Write this amount as a number.

3   Arrange these numbers in descending order.

    6 782 149   6 812 993   582 107   696 999

4   Oliver has 3347 songs on his MP3 player.
    Angelina has 3425 songs on her MP3 player.

    Who has the most songs on their MP3 player?

5   Arthur is on floor 3 of a building.
    He takes the lift down 7 floors.

    a)   Which floor is Arthur on now?

    b)   Vincent is 2 floors below Arthur.
        Which floor is Vincent on?

6   It is –6 °C outside a castle. It is 5 °C inside the castle.

    What is the difference in temperature between outside and inside the castle?

7   Colin says that –7 + 8 = –15. Is he correct?

    Explain your answer.

Practice Questions

8   Marietta is doing some history homework. She finds this table which tells her when certain towns were founded.

a) What year was Buckhead founded?

b) Was Roswell founded before or after Buckhead?

Town	Year Founded
Buckhead	MLXVI
Roswell	MMIII

9   Dean eats 3.562 kg of spaghetti.

a) What is the value of the 6 in this number?

b) What is the value of the 2 in this number?

10   Arrange these numbers from smallest to largest.

     12.25   8.4   8.32   8.104   12.3

11   In one day, Lee cycled 68.35 km and Fred cycled 68.306 km.

   Who cycled the furthest?

12   Round 8 523 419 to the nearest:

a) hundred   b) ten thousand   c) million

13   Parvati's backpack weighs 1.62 kg.

   Round the weight of her backpack to the nearest whole number.

14   Cho throws a shot put 7.236 m.

   Round this distance to 1 decimal place.

Written Adding and Subtracting

You Should Add In Columns

TTh Th H T U
```
  6 2 3 9 1
+ 1 4 8 1 7
```

EXAMPLE: Work out <u>62 391 + 14 817</u>

First, write the numbers on top of each other with the units lined up.

① Add the <u>UNITS</u> column first.

```
TTh Th H T U
   6 2 3 9 1
 + 1 4 8 1 7
 _____
           8
```

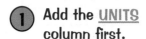

> You add decimals in the same way — just line up the decimal points and add in zeros (see below).

② Add the <u>TENS</u> column next.

```
TTh Th H T U
   6 2 3 9 1
 + 1 4 8 1 7
 _____
          0 8
         1
```

| 9 + 1 = 10 |

The <u>0</u> goes in the <u>tens</u> space.

10 tens = 100. So carry 100 to the hundreds column.

③ Then the <u>HUNDREDS</u>.

```
TTh Th H T U
   6 2 3 9 1
 + 1 4 8 1 7
 _____
         2 0 8
        1 1
```

| 3 + 8 + 1 = 12 |

The <u>2</u> goes in the <u>hundreds</u> space.

10 hundreds = 1000. So carry 1000 to the thousands column.

④ Add the <u>THOUSANDS</u> and <u>TEN THOUSANDS</u>.

```
TTh Th H T U
   6 2 3 9 1
 + 1 4 8 1 7
 _____
   7 7 2 0 8
        1 1
```

| 2 + 4 + 1 = 7 |

| 6 + 1 = 7 |

So 62 391 + 14 817 = <u>77 208</u>

In Subtractions, You May Need to Exchange

You set out <u>subtractions</u> the same as additions. Line up the <u>units</u> or decimal points. Then you start subtracting with the column of <u>least place value</u>.

EXAMPLE: Work out <u>51.4 − 12.37</u>

Add a <u>zero</u> to 51.4 so each number has the same number of decimal places.

Start by lining up the decimal points.

① Subtract the <u>HUNDREDTHS</u>.

```
T U . t h
5 1 . 4³ 0¹
− 1 2 . 3 7
_____
        . 3
```

You can't do 0 − 7, so exchange one of the <u>tenths</u> for 10 <u>hundredths</u>. There's <u>one tenth</u> less in the tenths column, so this becomes 4 − 1 = 3.

| 10 − 7 = 3 |

② Subtract the <u>TENTHS</u>.

```
T U . t h
5 1 . 4³ 0¹
− 1 2 . 3 7
_____
        . 0 3
```

| 3 − 3 = 0 |

③ Subtract the <u>UNITS</u>.

```
T  U . t  h
⁴5 ¹1 . 4³ 0¹
−  1 2 . 3 7
_____
   9 . 0 3
```

You can't do 1 − 2, so exchange one of the <u>tens</u> for 10 <u>units</u>. There's <u>one ten</u> less in the tens column, so this becomes 5 − 1 = 4.

| 11 − 2 = 9 |

④ Subtract the <u>TENS</u>.

```
T  U . t  h
⁴5 ¹1 . 4³ 0¹
−  1 2 . 3 7
_____
  3 9 . 0 3
```

| 4 − 1 = 3 |

So 51.4 − 12.37 = <u>39.03</u>

"I can use standard written methods to add and subtract numbers."

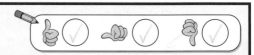

Worked Examples

1 Alastair bought a new phone for **£89.95** and a phone case for **£6.27**.
How much did he spend in total?

1) Start by writing the numbers on top of each other. Make sure you <u>line up</u> the <u>decimal points</u>.

2) Add from <u>right</u> to <u>left</u>, adding the <u>hundredths</u> first. **7 + 5 = 12**, so <u>carry</u> 10 hundredths = one tenth to the tenths column.

3) Next, add the <u>tenths</u>. **9 + 2 + 1 = 12**, so <u>carry</u> 10 tenths = one unit to the <u>units</u> column.

4) Now add the <u>units</u>. **9 + 6 + 1 = 16**, so <u>carry</u> 10 units = one ten to the <u>tens</u> column.

5) Finally, add up the <u>tens</u>.

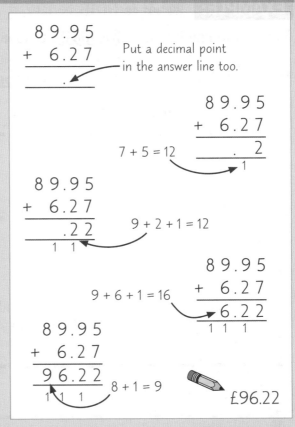

```
  8 9.9 5
+   6.2 7
_____
        .
```
Put a decimal point in the answer line too.

```
  8 9.9 5
+   6.2 7
_____
        . 2
          1
```
7 + 5 = 12

```
  8 9.9 5
+   6.2 7
_____
      . 2 2
      1 1
```
9 + 2 + 1 = 12

```
  8 9.9 5
+   6.2 7
_____
    6.2 2
    1 1 1
```
9 + 6 + 1 = 16

```
  8 9.9 5
+   6.2 7
_____
  9 6.2 2
  1 1 1
```
8 + 1 = 9

£96.22

2 Work out **6024 – 3753**.

```
  6 0 2 4
- 3 7 5 3
_____
        1
```

Exchange one of the thousands for ten hundreds. You're left with 6 – 1 = 5 thousands.

```
      5 10
  6̶ 0̶ 2 4
- 3 7 5 3
_____
        1
```

```
    9
  5 1̶0̶ 1
  6̶ 0̶ 2 4
- 3 7 5 3
_____
  2 2 7 1
```

2271

1) <u>Line up</u> the numbers on top of each other and start subtracting from <u>right</u> to <u>left</u>. First subtract the <u>units</u>.

2) Now subtract the <u>tens</u>. You can't do **2 – 5** in the tens column. There are <u>no hundreds</u> to exchange for 10 tens so exchange <u>one thousand</u> for <u>10 hundreds</u>.

3) Then exchange a <u>one hundred</u> for <u>10 tens</u>, so you have <u>9 hundreds</u> left.

4) Finish the rest of the subtraction.

Keep those pesky decimals in line...

When adding and subtracting decimals in columns, remember to line up the decimal points. You might even have to add extra zeros on the end of some of your numbers.

Written Multiplication

Long Multiplication

EXAMPLE: What is 3015 × 13?

You're multiplying by a <u>two-digit</u> number.
This looks tricky but all you need to do is <u>partition</u> this number: 13 = 10 + 3.
Work out 3015 × 10 and 3015 × 3 <u>separately</u>, then <u>add them together</u>.

1 First find 3015 × 3

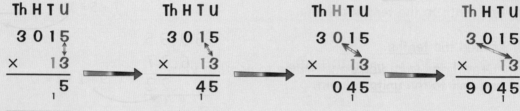

Th H T U	Th H T U	Th H T U	Th H T U
3 0 1 5	3 0 1 5	3 0 1 5	3 0 1 5
× 1 3	× 1 3	× 1 3	× 1 3
5	4 5	0 4 5	9 0 4 5

5 × 3 = 15	**1 × 3 = 3**	**0 × 3 = 0**	**3 × 3 = 9**
So put 5 in the U column, and carry the 1 to the T column.	Don't forget to add the 1, and write it in the T column.		

2 Now find 3015 × 10

Th H T U	Th H T U	Th H T U	Th H T U
3 0 1 5	3 0 1 5	3 0 1 5	3 0 1 5
× 1 3	× 1 3	× 1 3	× 1 3
9 0 4 5	9 0 4 5	9 0 4 5	9 0 4 5
5 0	1 5 0	0 1 5 0	3 0 1 5 0

5 × 10 = 50	**1 × 10 = 10**	**0 × 10 = 0**	**3 × 10 = 30**
So put 50 in the correct columns.	Write the 1 in the H column.	Write the 0 in the Th column.	Finish by putting 3 in the correct column.

3 Add to get the final answer.

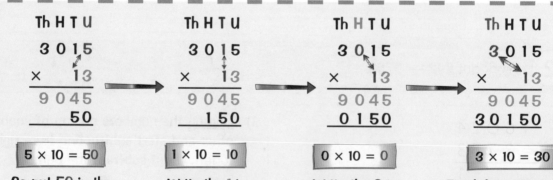

So 3015 × 13 = **39 195**

```
  Th H T U
   3 0 1 5
 ×    1 3
   9 0 4 5     This is your answer from Step 1.
+3 0 1 5 0     This is your answer from Step 2.
 3 9 1 9 5
```

"I can multiply a four-digit number by a two-digit number."

Worked Examples

1) Multiply **1234 × 23**.

1) Write the smaller number under the bigger number and <u>line up</u> the columns.

2) Work out <u>1234 × 3</u>, working from right to left. If you get 10 or more in a column, <u>carry</u> the first digit to the next column.

3) Work out <u>1234 × 20</u> on the next row, working from <u>right</u> to <u>left</u>.

4) <u>Add</u> the two rows together.

```
  1 2 3 4
×     2 3
```

E.g. 4 × 3 = 12, so write 2 in the units column and carry the 1.

```
  1 2 3 4
×     2 3
  3 7 0 2
    1 1
```

Then 3 × 3 = 9, plus the carried 1 gives 10.

```
  1 2 3 4
×     2 3
  3 7 0 2
+2 4 6 8 0
 2 8 3 8 2
      1
```

28 382

2) Barney travels **7342** miles each month. How many miles does he travel in a year?

```
    7 3 4 2
  ×     1 2
```

```
  7 3 4 2
×     1 2
1 4 6 8 4
```

```
    7 3 4 2
  ×     1 2
  1 4 6 8 4
  7 3 4 2 0
```

```
  7 3 4 2
×     1 2
1 4 6 8 4
+7 3 4 2 0
 8 8 1 0 4
    1 1
```

88 104 miles

1) There are <u>12 months</u> in a year, so you need to <u>multiply</u> 7342 by 12. Write the smaller number under the bigger number and <u>line up</u> the columns.

2) Work out <u>7342 × 2</u>, working from <u>right</u> to <u>left</u>. If you get 10 or more in a column, <u>carry</u> the first digit to the next column.

3) Now work out <u>7342 × 10</u> on the next row, working from <u>right</u> to <u>left</u>.

4) <u>Add</u> the two rows together.

<u>*My multiplication is 15 metres long...*</u>

Long multiplication is a really useful thing to know how to do. There are a few different steps to it, but this makes the calculation easier. I promise.

Written Division

Short Division

This method is good for dividing by fairly <u>small</u> numbers.

1) <u>Partition</u> the big number into thousands, hundreds, tens and units. Divide each of these numbers, starting with the <u>highest</u> place value.

2) Put the <u>result</u> of each division <u>on top</u> in the correct place value column.

3) Sometimes you need to <u>exchange</u>. This example shows you how.

EXAMPLE: What is 2472 ÷ 12?

If the numbers don't divide exactly you'll have a left-over, so you'll have to do some exchanging. You can see this on the next page.

$$12 \overline{| 2^2 4\ 7\ 2}$$

2472 = 2000 + 472
2 thousands don't divide by 12 to give any thousands, so exchange the 2 thousands for 20 hundreds.

$$12 \overline{| 2^2 4\ 7\ 2} \quad \overset{2}{}$$

You've got 24 in the hundreds place. 24 divides by 12:

$$24 \div 12 = 2$$

So put 2 on top in the hundreds place.

$$12 \overline{| 2\ 4\ 7^7 2} \quad \overset{20}{}$$

7 tens don't divide by 12 to give any tens, so put 0 on top in the tens place and exchange the 7 tens for 70 units.

$$12 \overline{| 2\ 4\ 7^7 2} \quad \overset{206}{}$$

You've got 72 units.

$$72 \div 12 = 6$$

So put 6 on top in the units place.

2472 ÷ 12 = <u>206</u>

The Remainder is the Bit Left Over

Sometimes one number won't divide perfectly by another.
The amount <u>left over</u> after the division is called the <u>remainder</u>.

EXAMPLE: 10 into 53 goes <u>5 times with remainder 3</u> (because 5 × 10 = 50)

You can write the remainder as a <u>number</u>, a <u>fraction</u> or a <u>decimal</u>.

So $53 \div 10 = 5\ r\ 3 = 5\frac{3}{10} = 5.3$

The number on the bottom of the fraction needs to be the number you were <u>dividing</u> by.

Sometimes you'll need to round the answer to a whole number.

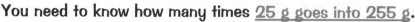

EXAMPLE: Mary's berry cake uses 25 g of raspberries. She has 255 g of raspberries. How many cakes can she bake?

You need to know how many times <u>25 g goes into 255 g</u>.

255 ÷ 25

$$25 \overline{| 2\ ^2 5\ 5} \quad \overset{1\ 0\ r\ 5}{}$$

Mary can't bake a cake with only 5 g of raspberries so <u>ignore</u> the remainder.

So Mary can bake <u>10 cakes</u>.

"I can divide a four-digit number by a two-digit number and know what to do with remainders."

Worked Examples

(1) Work out **7584 ÷ 4**.

1) Start by finding how many times <u>4</u> goes into <u>7</u>.

2) The answer is 1 r 3. Put the <u>1</u> on top in the thousands place, and <u>exchange</u> the 3 left-over thousands for <u>30 hundreds</u>. Now you have 35 hundreds.

2) <u>35</u> is in the <u>hundreds</u> place. 35 ÷ 4 = 8 r 3, so write <u>8</u> on top in the hundreds place, and <u>exchange</u> the 3 hundreds for <u>30 tens</u>.

3) <u>38</u> is now in the <u>tens</u> place. 38 ÷ 4 = 9 r 2, so write <u>9</u> on top in the tens place, and <u>exchange</u> the 2 tens for <u>20 units</u>.

4) <u>24</u> is now in the <u>units</u> place. 24 divides by 4 exactly, so there is <u>no remainder</u>.

$$\begin{array}{r} 1 \\ 4\overline{)7\,^3584} \end{array}$$

$$\begin{array}{r} 1\;8 \\ 4\overline{)7\,^35\,^384} \end{array}$$

$$\begin{array}{r} 1\;8\;9 \\ 4\overline{)7\,^35\,^38\,^24} \end{array}$$

$$\begin{array}{r} 1\;8\;9\;6 \\ 4\overline{)7\,^35\,^38\,^24} \end{array}$$ → 1896

---

(2) Paul divides **359** books equally into **11** boxes. How many books are left over?

1) 11 doesn't go into 3, so <u>exchange</u> the <u>3 hundreds</u> for <u>30 tens</u>.

2) 35 is in the <u>tens</u> place. 35 ÷ 11 = 3 r 2, so write <u>3</u> on top in the tens place, and <u>exchange</u> the <u>2 tens</u> that are left over for <u>20 units</u>.

3) 29 is now in the <u>units</u> place. 29 ÷ 11 = 2 r 7, so write <u>2</u> on top in the units place.

4) 7 is the <u>remainder</u>. Paul can put 32 books into each box, but he'll have 7 books left over.

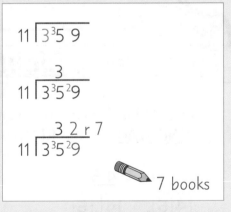

$$11\overline{)3\,^359}$$

$$\begin{array}{r} 3 \\ 11\overline{)3\,^35\,^29} \end{array}$$

$$\begin{array}{r} 3\;2\;r\;7 \\ 11\overline{)3\,^35\,^29} \end{array}$$ → 7 books

---

(3) Work out **67 ÷ 10**. Give your answer as a **mixed number**.

$$6\;r\;7 \;=\; 6\tfrac{7}{10}$$

1) 10 into 67 goes <u>6 times with remainder 7</u> (because 6 × 10 = 60).

2) Write this as a <u>mixed number</u>.

Leftovers are always tasty the next day...

Short division is really handy, but don't forget about remainders too. You might be told how to write the remainder, or you might have to round up or down.

Multiplying & Dividing by 10, 100 & 1000

Move Digits Left to Multiply by 10, 100 or 1000

If you're multiplying by 10, move the digits ONE PLACE to the LEFT.

$68 \times 10 = \underline{680}$

| | 6 | 8 | . |
| | 6 | 8 | 0 | . |

Add a decimal point if there isn't one.

Fill in empty places before the decimal point with zeros.

If you multiply by 100, move the digits TWO PLACES to the LEFT.

(The number of zeros tells you the number of places to move.)

$43.2 \times 100 = \underline{4320}$

| | | 4 | 3 | . | 2 |

| 4 | 3 | 2 | 0 | . | 0 |

| 4 | 3 | 2 | 0 |

Add a zero in here.

There's no need to add zeros after the decimal point.

If you multiply by 1000, move the digits THREE PLACES to the LEFT.

$17.9 \times 1000 = \underline{17\ 900}$

| | | | 1 | 7 | . | 9 |

| 1 | 7 | 9 | 0 | 0 | . | 0 |

| 1 | 7 | 9 | 0 | 0 |

You don't need a zero here.

The two gaps before the decimal point need to be filled in with zeros.

Move Digits Right to Divide by 10, 100 or 1000

To divide by 10 move the digits ONE PLACE to the RIGHT.

$45 \div 10 = \underline{4.5}$

| 4 | 5 | . |

| 4 | . | 5 |

You need to put a decimal point here.

You might have to add or remove zeros.

To divide by 100 move the digits TWO PLACES to the RIGHT.

$3.6 \div 100 = \underline{0.036}$

| 3 | . | 6 | | |

| | . | | 3 | 6 |

| 0 | . | 0 | 3 | 6 |

Fill in the gaps with zeros.

To divide by 1000 move the digits THREE PLACES to the RIGHT.

$700 \div 1000 = \underline{0.7}$

| 7 | 0 | 0 | . | | | |

| | | | . | 7 | 0 | 0 |

| | 0 | . | 7 | |

Add a decimal point.

Add a zero at the start.

You can remove these zeros.

"I can multiply or divide numbers by 10, 100 or 1000."

Worked Examples

1   Work out **63.54 × 1000**.

1) You're multiplying by <u>1000</u>, so move the digits <u>three places</u> to the <u>left</u>.

2) Fill up the empty place before the decimal point with a <u>zero</u>.

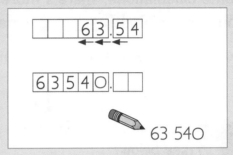

63 540

2   A single daffodil bulb costs **54p**. Rimi buys **10** daffodil bulbs. How much does she spend on daffodil bulbs in total? Give your answer in **pounds**.

Rimi spends £5.40

1) You're multiplying by <u>10</u>, so move the digits <u>one place</u> to the <u>left</u>.

2) Fill up the empty place before the decimal point with a <u>zero</u>.

3) <u>100p = £1</u>, so <u>divide</u> your answer by <u>100</u>. Move the digits <u>two places</u> to the <u>right</u>.

3   Calculate **8.4 ÷ 100**.

1) You're dividing by <u>100</u>, so move the digits <u>two places</u> to the <u>right</u>.

2) Fill up the empty places at the start with <u>zeros</u>.

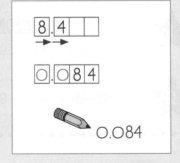

0.084

Ten things I like about Maths...

Don't forget — move the digits **LEFT** when multiplying and **RIGHT** when dividing. The numbers get bigger when multiplying and smaller when dividing. Simple.

Order of Operations

Always do Calculations in a Certain Order

In some calculations, there's more than one thing to do.
If you want to find <u>8 – 1 × 2</u>, what do you do <u>first</u>? Subtract or multiply?

Luckily, there's a rule that tells you the order to do things: BODMAS

B	O	D	M	A	S
Brackets (see below)		Division	Multiplication	Addition	Subtraction

So for 8 – 1 × 2, you'd do the
<u>multiplication first</u>, then the subtraction.

Answer: 8 – 2 = <u>6</u>

Brackets tell you which Step to do First

Some number sentences have <u>brackets</u> in.
The brackets show you which bit to do <u>first</u>.

10 ÷ (2 + 3) = ?   This means do the <u>addition first</u>: 2 + 3 = 5
Then do the <u>division</u>: 10 ÷ 5 = **2**

Always Follow the BODMAS Rules

Make sure you <u>read the question</u> carefully.

EXAMPLE: Stu works out 12 – (3 + 6) ÷ 3 = 1. Is Stu correct?
Explain your answer.

1 Remember the <u>BODMAS</u> rules.
Work out the <u>brackets</u> first.   12 – (3 + 6) ÷ 3 = 12 – 9 ÷ 3

2 Now <u>divide</u>...   12 – 9 ÷ 3 = 12 – 3   **3** ...then <u>subtract</u>.   12 – 3 = 9

Stu is <u>INCORRECT</u>. The correct answer is <u>9</u>.

"I know the order to do things in a calculation."

Worked Examples

1 Work out **5 × (4 − 1)**.

1) BODMAS says to do the <u>brackets</u> first.

2) Now work out the <u>multiplication</u>.

$5 \times (4 - 1) = 5 \times 3 \longleftarrow 4 - 1 = 3$

 $= 15$

2 Which of the following is correct?
6 − 4 + 1 = 1   (6 − 4) + 1 = 1   6 − (4 + 1) = 1

1) Work out the <u>first</u> calculation. It doesn't equal 1, so this is <u>incorrect</u>.

2) Now work out the <u>second</u> calculation. BODMAS says work out the brackets first, then add. It doesn't equal 1, so this is <u>incorrect</u>.

3) Finally, work out the <u>last</u> calculation. Work out the <u>brackets first</u>. Then <u>subtract</u> from 6.

$6 - 4 + 1 = 3$

$(6 - 4) + 1 = 2 + 1 \qquad 6 - 4 = 2$
$\qquad\qquad = 3$

$6 - (4 + 1) = 6 - 5 \longleftarrow 4 + 1 = 5$
$\qquad\qquad = 1$

 The correct calculation is
$6 - (4 + 1) = 1$

3 Work out **36 ÷ (4 + 5) × 2**.

$36 \div (4 + 5) \times 2 = 36 \div 9 \times 2$
$\qquad\qquad\qquad 4 + 5 = 9$

$36 \div 9 \times 2 = 4 \times 2$
$\qquad\qquad 36 \div 9 = 4$

$4 \times 2 = 8$

 8

1) BODMAS says to do the <u>brackets</u> first.

2) Next, work out the <u>division</u>.

3) Then <u>multiply</u>.

In first place — the brackets...

When you're given a long maths calculation, remember the BODMAS rules.
If you just work from left to right, you might get the wrong answer.

Estimation and Accuracy

Round Numbers to Estimate Answers

If you need to make a <u>quick estimate</u>, a good way to do it is by <u>rounding</u>.

EXAMPLES: **1** Estimate: 43.98 – 21.84

To do a <u>quick estimation</u>, round each number to the nearest ten:

$$40 - 20 = \underline{20}$$

Or you could round to the nearest whole number.

44 and 22 are <u>nearer</u> the 'real' numbers than 40 and 20. So this is a <u>better estimate</u>.

$$44 - 22 = \underline{22}$$

2 Killian buys 3 beach balls for £4.12 each. Harriet says that Killian spent £15.60 on beach balls. Use estimation to decide if she is correct.

Killian spent about <u>£12</u> on beach balls. So Harriet is <u>not correct</u>.

4.12 is close to 4, so round down. $\quad 4 \times 3 = \underline{12}$

You might have to use <u>different</u> rounding for <u>each number</u> to estimate your answer.

EXAMPLE: A 585 g box of Whizzing Wheetio Cereal contains 18 servings. Estimate how much cereal you get in a serving.

The <u>exact</u> size of a serving is 585 ÷ 18. $\qquad 600 \div 20 = \underline{30\text{ g}}$

Round this to the nearest 100.

Round this to the nearest 10.

Always round to numbers that make the calculation nice and easy.

Check that Your Answer is Sensible

It's easy to make mistakes. Always <u>read your answer</u> and see if it <u>makes sense</u>.

"The <u>giraffe</u> is <u>5 m</u> tall." ◀— This is <u>OK</u>.

"The <u>bus</u> is <u>2 mm</u> long." ◀— This <u>can't be right</u>. You don't get 2 mm long buses.

"I can estimate to check the answer to a calculation."

Worked Examples

---

1 Cat drinks **2.8 litres** of water every day.
Estimate how much water she drinks over **6** days.

1) <u>Write down</u> the calculation.

2) Now <u>round</u> 2.8 to the nearest whole number.

3) Use your <u>rounded value</u> to estimate the <u>answer</u>.

> 2.8 × 6
>
> 2.8 rounds up to 3
>
> 3 × 6 = 18
>
> 18 litres

---

2 **1 kg** of flour costs **£2.17**. Matt wants to buy **3.6 kg** of flour. Matt has **£5**. He thinks that this is enough to buy the flour he wants. Is Matt correct?

1) <u>Write down</u> the calculation.

2) Now <u>round</u> 2.17 and 3.3 to the nearest whole numbers.

3) Use your <u>rounded values</u> to work out an <u>estimate</u> for the cost of the flour.

4) £8 is <u>more than £5</u>, so Matt doesn't have enough money.

> 2.17 × 3.6
>
> 2.17 rounds down to 2
>
> 3.6 rounds up to 4
>
> 2 × 4 = 8
>
> The flour will cost about £8.
>
> Matt is not correct.

---

3 Estimate the answer to **617 ÷ 19**.

> 617 rounds down to 600
>
> 19 rounds up to 20
>
> 600 ÷ 20 = 30
>
> 30

1) Choose how to round the numbers to make the calculation easy. First <u>round</u> 617 to the nearest <u>100</u>.

2) Now round 19 to the nearest <u>10</u>.

3) Use your <u>rounded values</u> to estimate the <u>answer</u>.

How many giraffes can you fit in a London bus?

When you're estimating, always use sensible numbers. For example, if you're estimating 111 × 2013, it's easier to do 100 × 2000 than 110 × 2010.

Multiples and Factors

Multiples are the Numbers in Times Tables

So the <u>multiples of 2</u> are just the numbers in the <u>2 times table</u>:

2   4   6   8   10   12   14   16   ...

It's easy to remember:
MULTIPLes are just
MULTIPLication tables.

| The <u>multiples of 6</u> are | 6 | 12 | 18 | 24 | 30 | 36 | ... |
| The <u>multiples of 9</u> are | 9 | 18 | 27 | 36 | 45 | 54 | ... |

Factors of a Number

The <u>factors</u> of a number are whole numbers that <u>divide exactly into</u> that number.

EXAMPLES:

The number 8 has factors 1, 8, 2 and 4 because $1 \times 8 = 8$ and $2 \times 4 = 8$

A number can be divided exactly by all of its factors.

The number 18 has factors 1, 18, 2, 9, 3 and 6 because $1 \times 18 = 18$, $2 \times 9 = 18$ and $3 \times 6 = 18$

1 and 2 are <u>common factors</u> of 8 and 18.

That means 8 and 18 <u>share</u> the factors 1 and 2.

EXAMPLE: Circle the numbers that have 4 as a common factor.

(16)   5   (24)   34   (20)

$4 \times 4 = 16$ $4 \times 6 = 24$ $4 \times 5 = 20$

Factors Come In Pairs

The <u>smallest factor</u> makes a pair with the <u>biggest one</u>, the <u>second smallest</u> makes a pair with the <u>second biggest</u>, and so on.

EXAMPLE: List the factor pairs of 15.

2 won't multiply by a whole number to make 15.

$1 \times 15 = 15$
$3 \times 5 = 15$

If you carry on like this, the next one would be 5×3... but that's the same as 3×5, so stop here.

So the factor pairs of 15 are <u>1 and 15</u>, <u>3 and 5</u>.

If there are an <u>odd</u> number of factors, the <u>middle factor</u> multiplies by <u>itself</u>. For example, the factors of 25 are 1, 5 and 25.

$1 \times 25 = 25$
$5 \times 5 = 25$

"I know how to find multiples, factors and common factors."

Worked Examples

(1) List the first five multiples of **7**.

Just write down the first five numbers
in the <u>7 times table</u>.

 7, 14, 21, 28, 35

(2) Which numbers in the box are **multiples** of **8**? | 24   12   18   40   8 |

 24, 40 and 8 are
all multiples of 8.

1) 8 <u>divides</u> into 24, 40 and 8 <u>exactly</u>,
so these <u>are</u> multiples of 8.

2) 8 <u>doesn't divide</u> into 12 or 18 <u>exactly</u>,
so these <u>aren't</u> multiples of 8.

(3) Find all the factor pairs of **24**.

1 × 24 = 24

2 × 12 = 24

3 × 8 = 24

4 × 6 = 24

 1 and 24, 2 and 12,
3 and 8, 4 and 6.

1) Start by writing down <u>1 × 24</u>.

2) Then try <u>2 × something</u> to make 24.

3) Carry on trying to make 24 by multiplying <u>pairs</u>
of numbers: 3 × something, 4 × something, etc.

4) Don't include a number if it <u>doesn't divide exactly</u>.

5) <u>Stop</u> when you get a <u>repeated</u> number
— here, it's **6**.

6) Write down all the <u>factor pairs</u>.

(4) Matt is thinking of a number between **35** and **45**.
8 is one of its factors and it is a multiple of **4**. What number is he thinking of?

1) List all the <u>multiples of 4</u> between **35** and **45**.

2) <u>40</u> is the only number to divide by 8 exactly,
so 8 is only a <u>factor</u> of 40.

36, 40, 44

40 ÷ 8 = 5   40

The factors went in two by two — hurrah...

It's easy to get multiples and factors mixed up, so just remember that MULTiples
comes from the MULTIPLication tables. They can go on for ever and ever and ever...

Prime Numbers

Prime Numbers Only Have Two Factors

A <u>prime number</u> is a number that has <u>exactly TWO FACTORS</u>: 1 and <u>itself</u>.

1) <u>1 is NOT a prime number</u> — it doesn't have exactly 2 factors.
2) All prime numbers end in <u>1, 3, 7 or 9</u>. <u>2 and 5 are the EXCEPTIONS</u>.
3) <u>2</u> is the only <u>even</u> prime.

> BUT not all numbers ending in 1, 3, 7 or 9 are prime. See below...

Check if a Number is a Prime Number

1) Does it end in 1, 3, 7 or 9 (or is it 2 or 5)?
2) Does it have any <u>factors</u> apart from itself and 1? If it has, it's not a prime.

EXAMPLE: I'm thinking of a prime number.
It's more than 60 but less than 65.
What is the number?

61 and 63 are the only numbers that end in <u>1</u>, <u>3</u>, <u>7</u> or <u>9</u>.

But 7 × 9 = 63, so it has factors other than itself and 1.

So the number must be <u>61</u>.

Here are the prime numbers up to 100.

```
 1  ②  ③  4  ⑤  6  ⑦  8  9  10
⑪ 12 ⑬ 14 15 16 ⑰ 18 ⑲ 20
21 22 ㉓ 24 25 26 27 28 ㉙ 30
㉛ 32 33 34 35 36 ㊲ 38 39 40
㊶ 42 ㊸ 44 45 46 ㊼ 48 49 50
51 52 ㊳ 54 55 56 57 58 ㊾ 60
㊶ 62 63 64 65 66 ㊻ 68 69 70
㉛ 72 ㊸ 74 75 76 77 78 ㊾ 80
81 82 ㊳ 84 85 86 87 88 ㊾ 90
91 92 93 94 95 96 ㊼ 98 99 100
```

Finding Prime Factors

<u>Whole numbers</u> that <u>aren't prime</u> are made up of <u>prime</u> numbers <u>multiplied together</u>. These prime numbers are called <u>prime factors</u>.

EXAMPLE: Which prime numbers multiply together to make 20?

All apart from 1.

1 Write down any factor pair of 20. $20 = 2 \times 10$

2 2 is a prime number, so it's a <u>prime factor</u> of 20. 10 <u>isn't</u> a prime (it's a <u>composite number</u>), so split it up into a factor pair.

$20 = 2 \times 2 \times 5$

10 = 2 × 5 and 2 and 5 are both prime.

Now <u>all</u> the factors are prime.

$20 = 2 \times 2 \times 5$

"I know how to find prime numbers and prime factors."

Worked Examples

1 Which of the numbers in the box are **prime**?

| 27 | 28 | 29 | 30 | 31 |

28 and 30 don't end in a 1, 3, 7 or 9. So they're not prime.

27 = 3 × 9, so 27 isn't prime.

29 has no factors other than 1 and 29

31 has no factors other than 1 and 31

 So the primes are 29 and 31.

1) Look at the <u>last digit</u>. Numbers ending in a <u>1</u>, <u>3</u>, <u>7</u> or <u>9</u> could be prime.

2) Now look for the <u>factors</u> of each remaining number.

3) If there are <u>no factors</u> other than itself and 1, the number <u>is prime</u>.

4) If you <u>can find</u> any other factors, then the number <u>isn't prime</u>.

---

2 Ceara and Micaela cannot agree. Ceara thinks 33 **is** a prime number and Micaela says it is **not** a prime number. Who is correct?

1) A prime number has <u>two factors</u> — <u>1</u> and <u>itself</u>.

2) The factors of **33** are <u>1</u>, <u>3</u>, <u>11</u> and <u>33</u>...

3) ...so it is <u>not</u> a prime number.

33 = 3 × 11, so 33 isn't prime

 Micaela is correct.

---

3 Write down all the **prime numbers** between **5** and **15**.

List all the numbers between 5 and 15 that have <u>exactly two factors</u>.

 7, 11, 13

---

4 Which **prime numbers** multiply together to make **42**?

42 = 6 × 7

6 = 2 × 3

42 = 2 × 3 × 7   2, 3 and 7

1) Write down any <u>factor pair</u> of 42.

2) <u>7</u> is a prime number. <u>6</u> isn't a prime number, so split this up into a factor pair.

3) <u>2</u> and <u>3</u> are both prime numbers.

All primed and ready for action...

You don't need to learn all the prime numbers, but it'd be a good idea to be able to spot all the ones up to 30. It'll make questions about primes a whole lot easier...

Square and Cube Numbers

Square Numbers

When you multiply a number by itself, you get a <u>square number</u>.
Here are the first few square numbers:

1	4	9	16	25	36	49	64	81	100	121	144 ...
(1×1)	(2×2)	(3×3)	(4×4)	(5×5)	(6×6)	(7×7)	(8×8)	(9×9)	(10×10)	(11×11)	(12×12)...

They're called <u>square numbers</u> because they are the areas in this pattern of <u>squares</u>.

$1 \times 1 = 1$

$2 \times 2 = 4$

$3 \times 3 = 9$
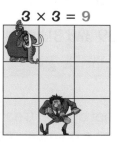

$4 \times 4 = 16$
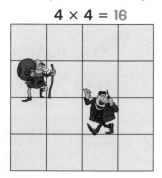

There's a quick way to write them.
You write <u>four squared</u> as 4^2.

EXAMPLES: $6^2 = 6$ squared $= 6 \times 6 = \underline{36}$
$13^2 = 13$ squared $= 13 \times 13 = \underline{169}$

Cube Numbers

You get a <u>cube number</u> by multiplying a number <u>by itself</u>, then <u>by itself again</u>.

EXAMPLES: 3 cubed $= 3 \times 3 \times 3 = \underline{27}$.   5 cubed $= 5 \times 5 \times 5 = \underline{125}$.

They're called <u>cube numbers</u> because they are the volumes in this pattern of cubes:

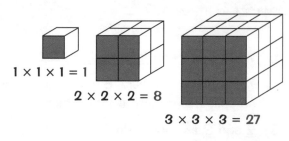
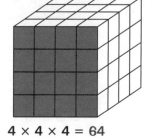

$1 \times 1 \times 1 = 1$
$2 \times 2 \times 2 = 8$
$3 \times 3 \times 3 = 27$
$4 \times 4 \times 4 = 64$

The quick way to write <u>three cubed</u> is 3^3.

"I can recognise and use square and cube numbers."

SECTION TWO — CALCULATIONS

Worked Examples

1 Find the next **square number**: 1, 4, 9, 16, 25, 36, 49, 64 ...

$9 \times 9 = 81$ 81

$64 = \underline{8 \times 8}$, so the next number in the sequence will be $\underline{9 \times 9}$.

2 Find two **square** numbers that **add** together to make **100**.

1) Make a <u>list</u> of the first few square numbers.

2) Find the two that <u>add</u> together to give <u>100</u>.

1, 4, 9, 16, 25, 36, 49, 64 ...

$36 + 64 = 100$

 36 and 64

3 List the next two **cube** numbers after **27**.

1) $27 = \underline{3 \times 3 \times 3}$, so the next cube number will be $\underline{4 \times 4 \times 4}$.

2) Then the next cube number will be $\underline{5 \times 5 \times 5}$.

$4 \times 4 \times 4 = 64$

$5 \times 5 \times 5 = 125$  64 and 125

4 Cyril says that $2^2 + 3^3 = 5^2$. Is he correct? Explain your answer.

$2^2 = 2 \times 2 = 4$

$3^3 = 3 \times 3 \times 3 = 27$

$27 + 4 = 31$

$5^2 = 5 \times 5 = 25$

 Cyril is not correct since 25 doesn't equal 31.

1) Start by working out $\underline{2^2}$. This is $\underline{2 \times 2}$.

2) Now work out $\underline{3^3}$. This is $\underline{3 \times 3 \times 3}$. <u>Add</u> your answer to 2^2.

3) Finally, work out $\underline{5^2}$. This is $\underline{5 \times 5}$.

4) Since 25 <u>doesn't equal</u> 31, Cyril is wrong.

Two squared, or not two squared...

Remember, for a square you multiply two lots of a number, and for a cube you multiply 3 lots. For example, $5^2 = 5 \times 5$ (two 5s) and $5^3 = 5 \times 5 \times 5$ (three 5s).

Practice Questions

1   Work out:

    a)   8475 + 4123   b)   51 432 + 7384   c)   68 754 – 4982

2   Rachel spends £65.84 on a suitcase, £4.23 on a book and £18.49 on sunglasses.

    How much does she spend in total?

3   Janice can run 800 m in 274.93 seconds.
    Emily can run 800 m 7.85 seconds quicker than Janice.

    How fast can Emily run 800 m?

4   Work out:

    a)   614 × 23   b)   2873 × 15

5   Monica is a chef. She cooks 4302 g of rice every day.

    How much rice does she cook in a week?

6   1368 people go up a mountain by cable car.
    Each cable car fits 12 people.

    How many cable cars were filled?

7   Calculate 2645 ÷ 7. Give your answer as:

    a)   a number with a remainder.

    b)   a mixed number.

8   Work out the missing number in each of these calculations:

    a)   .... × 100 = 3500   b)   0.24 × 10 = ...

    c)   6.74 × .... = 6740   d)   .... × 1000 = 59 820

Practice Questions

9   David cycled the same distance each day for 100 days.
    He cycled 6724 km in total.

    How far did he cycle each day?

10 Work out the following calculations:

    a) $16 - 4 \times 2 + 3$ b) $8 \times (6 - 1) + 12$

11 Ursula has 12 large books and 6 small books.
    She wants to divide her books equally between 3 shelves.

    Which of these calculations shows how many books will be on each shelf?

    $12 + 6 \div 3$ $12 + (6 \div 3)$ $(12 + 6) \div 3$

12 Estimate the answers to the following calculations:

    a) 6.4×8.2 b) $212 \div (4.1 \times 5.3)$

13 List the first 5 multiples of each of these numbers:

    a)   4   b)   12

14 Find all the factor pairs of:

    a)   30   b)   49

15 Find all the prime numbers between:

    a)   18 and 28   b)   58 and 68

16 Which prime numbers multiply together to make 18?

17 Gunther is thinking of a square number and a cube number.
    Together, they add up to 17.

    Which square and cube numbers is he thinking of?

Mixed Numbers and Improper Fractions

Improper Fractions and Mixed Numbers

An **IMPROPER** fraction is one where the numerator is bigger than the denominator.

Fractions with a smaller numerator than denominator are called **PROPER FRACTIONS**.

For example, $\frac{8}{3}$, $\frac{16}{5}$ and $\frac{18}{11}$ are all improper fractions.

MIXED NUMBERS have a whole number bit and a fraction bit — for example $2\frac{1}{3}$. You can change improper fractions into mixed numbers...

IMPROPER FRACTION $\frac{12}{7}$ ...is the same as... $1\frac{5}{7}$ MIXED NUMBER

We've got 12 sevenths. And 7 sevenths make up a whole.

So that means we've got one whole and 5 sevenths left over.

...and mixed numbers into improper fractions.

EXAMPLE: Write $3\frac{2}{5}$ as an improper fraction.

There are 5 fifths in a whole, so there are $3 \times 5 = 15$ fifths in 3.

So there are $15 + 2 = 17$ fifths in total, which means $3\frac{2}{5} = \frac{17}{5}$

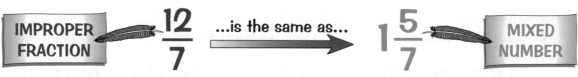

Using Improper Fractions and Mixed Numbers

To convert trickier improper fractions to mixed numbers, divide the numerator by the denominator. This gives you the whole-number part of the mixed number, and the remainder gives you the fraction part.

EXAMPLE: Luke makes some pizzas for a picnic. He cuts each one into 6 equal slices. At the end of the picnic he has 23 slices left. How many pizzas does he have left? Give your answer as a mixed number.

1) 1 slice = one sixth of a pizza. So the number of pizzas left as a fraction will have a denominator of 6.

2) There are 23 slices left. So the number of pizzas left is: $\frac{23}{6}$

There are 6 sixths in a whole.

3) Now write this as a mixed number — divide the numerator by the denominator: $23 \div 6 = 3$ remainder 5.

4) So there are 3 wholes with 5 sixths left over.

5) So the number of pizzas left is $\frac{23}{6} = 3\frac{5}{6}$

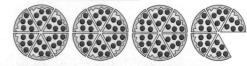

"I can swap between mixed numbers and improper fractions."

Worked Examples

1 Write $2\frac{3}{4}$ as an **improper fraction**.

There are 4 quarters in one whole, so there are 2 × 4 = 8 quarters in 2.

8 + 3 = 11

$2\frac{3}{4} = \frac{11}{4}$

1) Your fraction will have a <u>denominator</u> of <u>4</u>, so work out how many <u>quarters</u> there are in <u>2</u>.

2) Then <u>add on</u> the extra three quarters to find the <u>total number</u> of quarters.

3) Put this as the <u>numerator</u> and <u>4</u> as the <u>denominator</u>.

2 Write $\frac{22}{9}$ as a **mixed number**.

1) <u>Divide</u> the <u>numerator</u> by the <u>denominator</u>.

2) The answer tells you the <u>whole-number</u> part. The <u>remainder</u> tells you how many ninths are <u>left over</u> (the <u>fraction</u> part).

3) Put the two bits together to get your <u>answer</u>.

2 × 9 = 18, and 22 = 18 + 4, so 22 ÷ 9 = 2 remainder 4

So $\frac{22}{9}$ = 2 wholes with 4 ninths left over

$\frac{22}{9} = 2\frac{4}{9}$

3 Emmanuel, Richard and Dani each have a cake. Each cake has been cut into **12 identical slices**. Emmanuel has eaten **8** slices of his cake, Richard has eaten **6** slices of his cake and Dani has eaten **5** slices of her cake. How many cakes have been eaten **in total**? Give your answer as a **mixed number**.

1) Work out the <u>total</u> number of slices eaten. This is the <u>numerator</u>.

2) 1 slice = 1 twelfth of a cake, so the <u>denominator</u> will be <u>12</u>.

3) Divide <u>19</u> by <u>12</u> to convert the fraction to a <u>mixed number</u>.

4) Put the two bits together to get your <u>answer</u>.

8 + 6 + 5 = 19 slices

$\frac{19}{12}$ cakes eaten in total

19 ÷ 12 = 1 remainder 7

$1\frac{7}{12}$ cakes have been eaten in total.

My fractions are feeling a bit mixed up...

For mixed numbers and improper fractions, the denominator tells you how many parts there are in one whole. Use this to help you convert between them.

Comparing Fractions

Equivalent Fractions are Equal to Each Other

Equivalent fractions look different from each other, but are really the same.

For example $\frac{1}{2}$ and $\frac{4}{8}$ are equivalent fractions.

You can use fraction bars and see that the same amount is shaded.

You can calculate equivalent fractions too.

You just multiply or divide the numerator and denominator of a fraction by the same number.

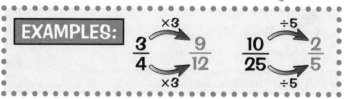

EXAMPLES:

$$\frac{3}{4} \xrightarrow{\times 3} \frac{9}{12} \qquad \frac{10}{25} \xrightarrow{\div 5} \frac{2}{5}$$

Putting Fractions in Size Order

If the denominators are the same, just compare the numerators.

The bigger the numerator, the bigger the fraction.

If the denominators are DIFFERENT, make them the same by finding equivalent fractions.

(Then compare the numerators.)

EXAMPLE: Put these fractions in order from smallest to largest: $\frac{5}{8}, \frac{7}{12}$ and $\frac{13}{24}$.

Step 1 Decide on a common denominator.
8, 12 and 24 all have 24 as a multiple, so use 24.

Step 2 Make equivalent fractions that have your common denominator.

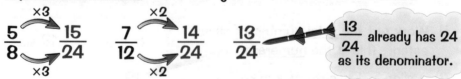

$$\frac{5}{8} \xrightarrow{\times 3} \frac{15}{24} \qquad \frac{7}{12} \xrightarrow{\times 2} \frac{14}{24} \qquad \frac{13}{24}$$

$\frac{13}{24}$ already has 24 as its denominator.

Step 3 Write out all the fractions and compare their numerators.

$$\frac{15}{24}, \frac{14}{24}, \frac{13}{24}$$

15 is larger than 14.
14 is larger than 13.

So from smallest to largest, the order is $\frac{13}{24}, \frac{14}{24}, \frac{15}{24}$

Now change the fractions back to the ones in the question: $\frac{13}{24}, \frac{7}{12}, \frac{5}{8}$

"I can compare and order fractions."

Worked Examples

1 Put these fractions in order from **smallest** to **largest**: $\frac{5}{12}, \frac{4}{9}, \frac{7}{18}$.

1) Find a <u>common denominator</u>. 12, 9 and 18 all have 36 as a multiple, so use <u>36</u>.

2) Find <u>equivalent fractions</u> that have 36 as a denominator.

3) Put the fractions in order by comparing the <u>numerators</u>.

4) Put each fraction back into its <u>original form</u>.

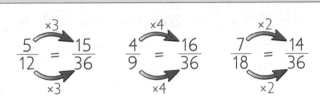

$$\frac{5}{12} \xrightarrow{\times 3} = \frac{15}{36} \quad \frac{4}{9} \xrightarrow{\times 4} = \frac{16}{36} \quad \frac{7}{18} \xrightarrow{\times 2} = \frac{14}{36}$$

$$\frac{14}{36}, \frac{15}{36}, \frac{16}{36}$$

So the order is: $\frac{7}{18}, \frac{5}{12}, \frac{4}{9}$

2 Chad, Ellie, Mike and Fay took part in a maths challenge.
The **fractions** of the questions that the children answered correctly were:
Chad: $\frac{3}{4}$, Ellie: $\frac{4}{5}$, Mike: $\frac{7}{10}$, Fay: $\frac{13}{20}$.
Work out who came **first**, **second**, **third** and **fourth** in the challenge.

Chad: $\frac{3}{4} \xrightarrow{\times 5} = \frac{15}{20}$ Ellie: $\frac{4}{5} \xrightarrow{\times 4} = \frac{16}{20}$

Mike: $\frac{7}{10} \xrightarrow{\times 2} = \frac{14}{20}$ Fay: $\frac{13}{20}$

$$\frac{16}{20}, \frac{15}{20}, \frac{14}{20}, \frac{13}{20}$$

So the order is:
1st = Ellie
2nd = Chad
3rd = Mike
4th = Fay

1) You have to order the fractions — so find a <u>common denominator</u>. 20 is a multiple of all four denominators, so use <u>20</u>.

2) Find <u>equivalent fractions</u> that have 20 as a denominator.

3) Put the fractions in order by comparing the <u>numerators</u>. Start with the <u>largest</u> to get the <u>highest score</u> first.

4) List the <u>children</u> in order (you <u>don't</u> need to put the fractions back into their original form to do this).

I love putting fractions in size order... $\frac{1}{8}, \frac{1}{4}, \frac{1}{2}$

If you're trying to put fractions in order, start by putting them over a common denominator. This is just a multiple of all the denominators.

Multiplying Fractions

Multiply Whole Numbers by Fractions...

When you're talking about fractions, "<u>of</u>" just means "<u>times</u>".

So calculating $\frac{1}{5} \times 20$ is the same as finding $\frac{1}{5}$ <u>of</u> 20.

> To multiply any number by a fraction, you <u>times</u> by the <u>numerator</u> and <u>divide</u> by the <u>denominator</u>.

EXAMPLE: What is $2\frac{5}{8} \times 16$?

1) <u>Partition</u> $2\frac{5}{8}$ into a <u>whole number</u> and a <u>fraction</u>: $2\frac{5}{8} = 2 + \frac{5}{8}$

2) <u>Multiply</u> the whole number by 16... $2 \times 16 = \underline{32}$

3) ... and <u>multiply</u> the fraction by 16.

$\frac{5}{8} \times 16$:

multiply by the numerator → $\dfrac{\mathbf{5}}{\mathbf{8}}$

divide by the denominator →

$16 \div 8 = 2$

$2 \times 5 = \underline{10}$

It doesn't matter what order you do it in — just do what's easier.

4) <u>Add</u> the two answers together. $32 + 10 = \underline{42}$ So $2\frac{5}{8} \times 16 = \underline{42}$.

...Or Fractions by Other Fractions

To <u>multiply fractions</u>:

> 1) <u>Multiply</u> the <u>top numbers</u>.
> 2) <u>Multiply</u> the <u>bottom numbers</u>.

$3 \times 1 = 3$

$\frac{3}{4} \times \frac{1}{5} = \frac{3}{20}$

$4 \times 5 = 20$

EXAMPLE: What is $\frac{1}{2} \times \frac{1}{2}$? ← That's a half <u>of</u> a half.

Multiply the <u>numerators together</u> and multiply the <u>denominators together</u>: $\frac{1}{2} \times \frac{1}{2} = \frac{1 \times 1}{2 \times 2}$ and the answer is $\frac{1}{4}$.

Here it's shown on a <u>fraction bar</u>:

$\frac{1}{2}$ $\frac{1}{2} \times \frac{1}{2} = \frac{1}{4}$

You'll notice the answer's <u>smaller</u>, even though you're <u>multiplying</u>. Imagine <u>half</u> a cake being cut <u>in half</u> — you get a <u>quarter</u> of a cake.

"I can multiply fractions by whole numbers, and by other fractions."

Worked Examples

1 Calculate $\frac{5}{6}$ × 24.

$24 \div 6 = 4$

$4 \times 5 = 20$

1) For this one, it's easier to <u>divide</u> by the <u>denominator</u> first — so do $\underline{24 \div 6}$.

2) Then <u>multiply</u> this value by the <u>numerator</u> — so do $\underline{4 \times 5}$ (this is the answer).

2 What is $4\frac{2}{5}$ × 15?

1) Start by <u>partitioning</u> $4\frac{2}{5}$ into a <u>fraction</u> and a <u>whole number</u>.

2) Multiply the <u>whole number</u> part by <u>15</u>...

3) ...and multiply the <u>fraction</u> by 15 (<u>divide</u> by the <u>denominator</u> and <u>multiply</u> by the <u>numerator</u>).

4) <u>Add</u> the two parts to get the answer.

$4\frac{2}{5} = 4 + \frac{2}{5}$

$4 \times 15 = 60$

$\frac{2}{5} \times 15: 15 \div 5 = 3$

$3 \times 2 = 6$

$60 + 6 = 66$

3 What is $\frac{1}{2}$ × $\frac{1}{8}$?

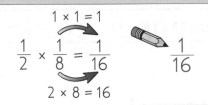

$\frac{1}{2} \times \frac{1}{8} = \frac{1}{16}$ $\qquad \frac{1}{16}$

$1 \times 1 = 1$

$2 \times 8 = 16$

1) Multiply the <u>top numbers</u>.

2) Multiply the <u>bottom numbers</u>.

4 What is $\frac{2}{3}$ × $\frac{7}{9}$?

1) Multiply the <u>top numbers</u>.

2) Multiply the <u>bottom numbers</u>.

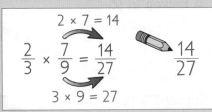

$\frac{2}{3} \times \frac{7}{9} = \frac{14}{27}$ $\qquad \frac{14}{27}$

$2 \times 7 = 14$

$3 \times 9 = 27$

But I don't want my cake to get smaller...

If you've forgotten which bit to multiply by and which bit to divide by, just remember that you <u>D</u>ivide by the <u>D</u>enominator (so you'll have to multiply by the numerator).

Adding and Subtracting Fractions

Fractions with the Same Denominator

When fractions have the same denominator, you can add or subtract their numerators.

EXAMPLE: What is $\frac{5}{9} + \frac{8}{9}$?

Add the two numerators together. →

The denominator stays the same. →

$$\frac{5}{9} + \frac{8}{9} = \frac{5+8}{9} = \frac{13}{9} \text{ or } 1\frac{4}{9}$$

Fractions with Different Denominators

If the denominators are not the same, you have to find a common denominator for your fractions first (see page 36).

Then you add or subtract the numerators only (as above).

EXAMPLE: What is $\frac{3}{4} - \frac{3}{10}$?

1) First find equivalent fractions with the same denominator for each.

20 is a multiple of 4 and 10, so use that as the common denominator.

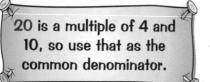

$$\frac{3}{4} \xrightarrow{\times 5} \frac{15}{20} \qquad \frac{3}{10} \xrightarrow{\times 2} \frac{6}{20}$$

2) Subtract the numerators to get the answer:
$$\frac{3}{4} - \frac{3}{10} = \frac{15}{20} - \frac{6}{20} = \frac{15-6}{20} = \frac{9}{20}$$

Change Mixed Numbers to Improper Fractions

EXAMPLE: Ed has $2\frac{1}{2}$ packets of sweets. Ruby gives him another $\frac{2}{3}$ of a packet. How many packets of sweets does he have now?

The calculation you have to do is $2\frac{1}{2} + \frac{2}{3}$.

Convert $2\frac{1}{2}$ to an improper fraction first.

There are $2 \times 2 = 4$ halves in 2, so there are $4 + 1 = 5$ halves in $2\frac{1}{2}$.

Now find equivalent fractions.
6 is a multiple of both 2 and 3, so use that for the denominator.

Now that the denominators are the same, you can add the numerators.

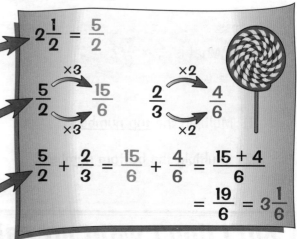

$$2\frac{1}{2} = \frac{5}{2}$$

$$\frac{5}{2} \xrightarrow{\times 3} \frac{15}{6} \qquad \frac{2}{3} \xrightarrow{\times 2} \frac{4}{6}$$

$$\frac{5}{2} + \frac{2}{3} = \frac{15}{6} + \frac{4}{6} = \frac{15+4}{6}$$

$$= \frac{19}{6} = 3\frac{1}{6}$$

"I can add and subtract fractions by finding equivalent fractions with the same denominator."

Worked Examples

1 Calculate $\frac{8}{11} + \frac{10}{11} - \frac{4}{11}$. Give your answer as a **mixed number**.

1) The denominators are the <u>same</u>,
   so just <u>add</u> and <u>subtract</u> the numerators.

2) Give your answer as a <u>mixed number</u>.
   $14 \div 11 = \underline{1\text{ remainder }3}$, so there's
   <u>1 whole</u> with <u>3 elevenths</u> left over.

$$\frac{8}{11} + \frac{10}{11} - \frac{4}{11} = \frac{8 + 10 - 4}{11}$$
$$= \frac{14}{11}$$

$$\frac{14}{11} = 1\frac{3}{11}$$

---

2 Robert has $\frac{3}{4}$ of a bar of chocolate. He eats $\frac{5}{8}$ of the bar.
How much chocolate does he have **left**?

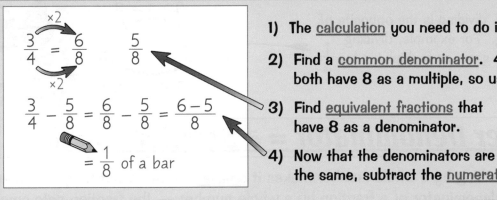

$$\frac{3}{4} = \frac{6}{8} \qquad \frac{5}{8}$$

$$\frac{3}{4} - \frac{5}{8} = \frac{6}{8} - \frac{5}{8} = \frac{6-5}{8}$$

$$= \frac{1}{8} \text{ of a bar}$$

1) The <u>calculation</u> you need to do is $\frac{3}{4} - \frac{5}{8}$.

2) Find a <u>common denominator</u>. 4 and 8
   both have 8 as a multiple, so use <u>8</u>.

3) Find <u>equivalent fractions</u> that
   have 8 as a denominator.

4) Now that the denominators are
   the same, subtract the <u>numerators</u>.

---

3 What is $1\frac{1}{6} + \frac{2}{9}$? Give your answer as an **improper fraction**.

$$1\frac{1}{6} = \frac{7}{6}$$

$$\frac{7}{6} = \frac{21}{18} \qquad \frac{2}{9} = \frac{4}{18}$$

$$\frac{7}{6} + \frac{2}{9} = \frac{21}{18} + \frac{4}{18} = \frac{21 + 4}{18}$$

$$= \frac{25}{18}$$

1) Convert $1\frac{1}{6}$ to an <u>improper fraction</u>.
   There are <u>6 sixths</u> in 1,
   so there are $\underline{6 + 1 = 7\text{ sixths}}$ in $1\frac{1}{6}$.

2) Find a <u>common denominator</u>. 6 and 9
   both have 18 as a multiple, so use <u>18</u>.

3) Find <u>equivalent fractions</u> that
   have 18 as a denominator.

4) Now that the denominators are
   the same, add the <u>numerators</u>.

Match your denominators to your shoes...

The most important thing to remember here is that you can only add or subtract
fractions if they have the same denominator. Otherwise it just won't work.

Dividing Fractions

Multiply The Denominator

Dividing fractions by whole numbers is easy if you know how.

To <u>divide</u> a <u>fraction</u> by a <u>whole number</u>, <u>multiply</u> the <u>denominator</u> by the whole number.

EXAMPLE: $\frac{3}{5} \div 4 = \frac{3}{20}$

$5 \times 4 = 20$

To <u>divide</u> a fraction by 4, take the <u>denominator</u> and <u>multiply</u> it by 4.

Remember, dividing is the opposite of multiplying. For example, dividing by 4 is the <u>same</u> as multiplying by $\frac{1}{4}$.

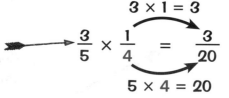

$3 \times 1 = 3$

$\frac{3}{5} \times \frac{1}{4} = \frac{3}{20}$

$5 \times 4 = 20$

A Bigger Denominator = a Smaller Fraction

<u>Dividing</u> something by a whole number makes it <u>smaller</u>. That's what happens when you <u>multiply</u> the <u>denominator</u> of a fraction by a whole number — the fraction <u>gets smaller</u>.

$\frac{1}{3} \div 4 = \frac{1}{12}$

$3 \times 4 = 12$

$\frac{3}{4} \div 2 = \frac{3}{8}$

$4 \times 2 = 8$

EXAMPLE:

Louise had $\frac{1}{2}$ of a carton of juice. She <u>divided</u> it equally into <u>3 cups</u>.

What fraction of a carton of juice is in each cup?

$\frac{1}{2} \div 3 = \frac{1}{6}$ So there is $\frac{1}{6}$ of a carton of juice in each cup.

$2 \times 3 = 6$

"I can divide fractions by whole numbers."

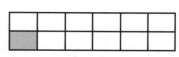

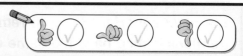

Worked Examples

1 Calculate $\frac{1}{7} \div 3$.

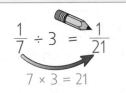

To divide a fraction by 3, you need to <u>multiply the denominator</u> by **3**.

2 Work out $\frac{3}{8} \div 10$.

To divide a fraction by 10, you need to <u>multiply the denominator</u> by **10**.

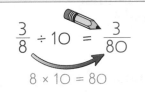

3 Angus cuts a pie into **quarters**. He then cuts each quarter into **4** equal pieces, and eats one of these pieces. What **fraction** of the pie has he eaten?

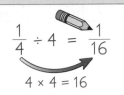

1) Angus divides each <u>quarter</u> into <u>4 pieces</u>, so you need to <u>divide one quarter by 4</u>.

2) To divide a fraction by 4, you need to <u>multiply the denominator</u> by **4**.

4 Farah has $\frac{9}{10}$ of a bag of popcorn.
She shares it out equally between **herself** and her **four sisters**.
What **fraction** of the bag of popcorn does each girl get?

1) Farah splits the fraction into <u>5 shares</u> (herself plus her four sisters), so you need to <u>divide it by 5</u>.

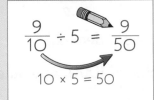

2) To divide a fraction by 5, you have to <u>multiply the denominator</u> by **5**.

Divide your fractions into two teams...

Remember — when you're dividing a fraction by a whole number, the answer should be smaller than the fraction you started with (so it'll have a bigger denominator).

Equivalent Fractions and Decimals

Find an Equivalent in Tenths or Hundredths or Thousandths...

You can <u>convert any fraction</u> to a <u>decimal</u>.

> If the <u>denominator</u> is a <u>factor</u> of <u>10</u>, <u>100</u> or <u>1000</u>,
> first find an <u>equivalent fraction</u> in tenths, hundredths or thousandths.
> Then, because $\frac{1}{10} = 0.1$, $\frac{1}{100} = 0.01$ and $\frac{1}{1000} = 0.001$,
> you know that, for example, $\frac{3}{10} = 0.3$, $\frac{9}{100} = 0.09$, and $\frac{17}{1000} = 0.017$.

To convert a decimal to a fraction, you need to look at the <u>tenths</u>, <u>hundredths</u> and <u>thousandths</u>.

> 1 tenth = 10 hundredths = 100 thousandths
> 1 hundredth = 10 thousandths

0.7   This decimal is <u>7 tenths</u> so it's equivalent to $\frac{7}{10}$.

0.49   This decimal is <u>4 tenths</u> and <u>9 hundredths</u>, which is the same as <u>49 hundredths</u>.
So it's equivalent to $\frac{49}{100}$.

0.347   This decimal is <u>3 tenths</u>, <u>4 hundredths</u> and <u>7 thousandths</u>. That's the same as <u>347 thousandths</u>.
So it's equivalent to $\frac{347}{1000}$.

EXAMPLES: 1) Write $\frac{13}{50}$ as a decimal.

50 is a factor of 100, so find an <u>equivalent fraction</u> in <u>hundredths</u>.

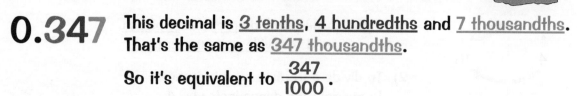

$\frac{13}{50} \xrightarrow{\times 2} \frac{26}{100}$ As $\frac{1}{100} = 0.01$, $\frac{26}{100} = 0.26$

2) Write $\frac{1}{250}$ as a decimal.

250 is a factor of 1000, so find an <u>equivalent fraction</u> in <u>thousandths</u>.

$\frac{1}{250} \xrightarrow{\times 4} \frac{4}{1000}$ As $\frac{1}{1000} = 0.001$, $\frac{4}{1000} = 0.004$

"I can convert between fractions and decimals."

45

Worked Examples

1 Circle the fraction below that is **equivalent** to 0.009.

The <u>9</u> is in the <u>thousandths</u> place,
so the decimal represents <u>nine thousandths</u>.

$\frac{9}{10}$ $\boxed{\frac{9}{1000}}$ $\frac{9}{100}$

2 Write 0.399 as a **fraction**.

$0.399 = \frac{399}{1000}$

1) This decimal is <u>3 tenths</u>, <u>9 hundreds</u> and <u>9 thousandths</u>. This is the same as <u>399 thousandths</u>.

2) So write <u>399</u> on the <u>top</u> of the fraction and <u>1000</u> on the <u>bottom</u>.

3 Write $\frac{709}{1000}$ as a **decimal**.

1) Use $\frac{1}{1000} = 0.001$ to write $\frac{709}{1000}$ as a <u>decimal</u>.

2) Make sure you put the <u>digits</u> in the right place. The <u>9</u> in 709 is <u>9 units</u>, so when you divide by 1000 it becomes <u>9 thousandths</u>, which is <u>0.009</u>.

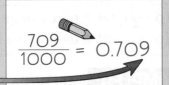

$\frac{709}{1000} = 0.709$

4 Convert $\frac{3}{20}$ to a **decimal**.

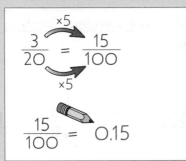

$\frac{3}{20} \overset{\times 5}{\underset{\times 5}{=}} \frac{15}{100}$

$\frac{15}{100} = 0.15$

1) 20 is a <u>factor of 100</u>, so find an <u>equivalent fraction</u> in hundredths.

2) Use $\frac{1}{100} = 0.01$ to write $\frac{15}{100}$ as a <u>decimal</u>.

Decorate cakes with hundredths and thousandths...

To convert a decimal to a fraction, put the digits after the decimal point over 10, 100 or 1000. To convert a fraction to a decimal, write it in 10ths, 100ths or 1000ths first.

Percentages

Useful Fractions, Decimals and Percentages...

You can write <u>any</u> fraction as a <u>percentage</u> as well as a <u>decimal</u>.
Here are some common ones you should know.

$\frac{1}{2}$ is the same as 50%, which is the same as 0.5

$\frac{1}{4}$ is the same as 25%, which is the same as 0.25

$\frac{3}{4}$ is the same as 75%, which is the same as 0.75

$\frac{1}{5}$ is the same as 20%, which is the same as 0.2

$\frac{2}{5}$ is the same as 40%, which is the same as 0.4

$\frac{4}{5}$ is the same as 80%, which is the same as 0.8

$\frac{1}{10}$ is the same as 10%, which is the same as 0.1

...and How to Convert Between Them

To convert a percentage to a decimal, <u>divide</u> by <u>100</u>.
To convert a decimal to a percentage, <u>multiply</u> by <u>100</u>.

Have a look at page 44 for how to convert between decimals and fractions.

EXAMPLES:

1) Write 22% as a decimal.

Just <u>divide</u> by 100: $22 \div 100 = \underline{0.22}$

2) Write 0.47 as a percentage.

Just <u>multiply</u> by 100: $0.47 \times 100 = \underline{47\%}$

To convert a fraction to a percentage, you need to make an <u>equivalent fraction</u> with <u>100 as the denominator</u>. The <u>numerator</u> is the percentage.

EXAMPLES:

$\overset{\times 10}{\frac{7}{10}} = \frac{70}{100} = \underline{70\%}$ (×10)　　　$\overset{\times 2}{\frac{23}{50}} = \frac{46}{100} = \underline{46\%}$ (×2)　　　$\overset{\times 4}{\frac{4}{25}} = \frac{16}{100} = \underline{16\%}$ (×4)

To convert a percentage to a fraction: 1) Turn the <u>percentage</u> into a <u>decimal</u>,
　　　　　　　　　　　　　　　2) Convert to a <u>fraction</u> (see page 44).

"I can convert between fractions,
decimals and percentages."

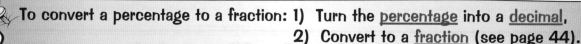

Worked Examples

1 Write 4% as a **decimal**.

$$4 \div 100 = 0.04$$

Divide the percentage by <u>100</u>.

2 Write 0.63 as a **percentage**.

Multiply the decimal by <u>100</u>.

$$0.63 \times 100 = 63\%$$

3 Noah is collecting football stickers. He has collected **148** stickers out of a total of **200**. What **percentage** of the total has he collected?

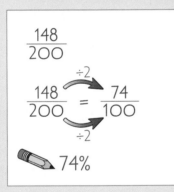

74%

1) Write the amount that Noah has collected as a <u>fraction</u>. The number he's collected (<u>148</u>) is the <u>numerator</u> and the total (<u>200</u>) is the <u>denominator</u>.

2) Make an <u>equivalent fraction</u> with <u>100</u> as the <u>denominator</u>.

3) The <u>numerator</u> is the <u>percentage</u> of stickers that Noah has collected.

4 Sita owns a taxi company. **87%** of the taxis are black. What **fraction** of the taxis are **not** black?

1) The whole set of taxis is <u>100%</u>. So the <u>percentage</u> of taxis that <u>aren't</u> black is **100%** <u>take away</u> **87%**.

2) Now you need to convert <u>13%</u> to a <u>fraction</u>. Start by turning it into a <u>decimal</u> (÷100).

3) Then turn the <u>decimal</u> into a <u>fraction</u>. This decimal is <u>one tenth</u> and <u>three hundredths</u>, which is the same as <u>thirteen hundredths</u>.

$$100\% - 87\% = 13\%$$

$$13 \div 100 = 0.13$$

$$0.13 = \frac{13}{100}$$

Well, you've certainly converted me...

Make sure you learn the common fractions, decimals and percentages on the previous page — it'll save you a lot of time if you don't have to work them out.

Practice Questions

1   Convert the fractions below.

   a)   Write $3\frac{3}{7}$ as an improper fraction.

   b)   Write $\frac{14}{5}$ as a mixed number.

2   Frankie, Kevin and Caroline each have a bar of chocolate divided into 10 equal pieces. Frankie has eaten 6 pieces of chocolate, Kevin has eaten 9 pieces of chocolate and Caroline has eaten 8 pieces of chocolate.

   How many chocolate bars have been eaten in total?
   Give your answer as a mixed number.

3   Which of the fractions below is equivalent to $\frac{5}{6}$?

   $\frac{6}{9}$ $\frac{10}{12}$ $\frac{15}{16}$ $\frac{20}{25}$ $\frac{9}{12}$

4   Put the fractions below in order from largest to smallest.

   $\frac{1}{2}$ $\frac{4}{9}$ $\frac{5}{6}$

5   Calculate the following:

   a) $\frac{2}{3} \times 21$ b) $2\frac{3}{5} \times 25$

6   Work out:

   a) $\frac{1}{3} \times \frac{1}{4}$ b) $\frac{3}{8} \times \frac{7}{10}$

7   For the calculations below, give your answers as mixed numbers.

   a) $\frac{8}{15} + \frac{11}{15} + \frac{4}{15}$

   b) $1\frac{9}{10} + \frac{3}{10} - \frac{1}{10}$

Practice Questions

8   Work out:

    a) $\frac{7}{8} - \frac{5}{12}$ b) $\frac{1}{3} + \frac{2}{7}$

9   Mark has $\frac{4}{5}$ of a tablespoon of jam.
He spreads $\frac{1}{4}$ of a tablespoon of jam on a piece of toast.

    What fraction of a tablespoon of jam does he have left?

10   Calculate:

    a) $\frac{1}{8} \div 4$

    b) $\frac{2}{5} \div 7$

11   Zahra cuts a loaf of bread into 5 equal pieces.
She then cuts each piece into 3 equal slices.

    What fraction of the whole loaf is one slice of bread?

12   Convert:

    a)   0.219 to a fraction.   b)   0.49 to a fraction.

    c) $\frac{16}{25}$ to a decimal.   d) $\frac{3}{500}$ to a decimal.

13   Write:

    a)   0.39 as a percentage.   b)   13% as a decimal.

14   Justin has 50 T-shirts. 11 of the T-shirts are white.

    What percentage of his T-shirts are white?

15   60% of Scott's friends are at his birthday party.

    What fraction of his friends are **not** at his birthday party?

Ratio and Proportion

Use Scaling to Solve Money Problems

Scaling up and down is all about multiplying and dividing.

EXAMPLE: One bottle of carrot juice costs 19p. How much will five bottles cost?

19p   **19p × 5**   95p

So five bottles of carrot juice cost 95p.

ANOTHER EXAMPLE: In a different shop you can buy six bottles of carrot juice for 90p. How much will four bottles cost?

First you need to divide by 6 to find out how much 1 bottle costs: 90p ÷ 6 = 15p

Then you need to multiply by 4 to find the cost of 4 bottles: 15p × 4 = 60p

So four bottles of carrot juice cost 60p.

Ratios Compare One Part to Another Part

Look at this pattern:

For the 2 white squares there are 4 pink squares.
So for every white square there are 2 pink squares.
As a ratio, this is 1:2 — you'd say "1 white to 2 pink".

You can use ratios to solve problems.

EXAMPLE: Dave's shop is offering 1 free turtle with every 3 skateboards bought. I buy 15 skateboards. How many free turtles will I get?

The ratio is 3 skateboards to 1 turtle (3:1).
15 skateboards is 5 lots of 3 skateboards.

So I get 5 lots of 1 free turtle.
5 × 1 = 5 free turtles.

3 skateboards get... 1 turtle
×5   ×5
15 skateboards get... ? turtles

"I can solve problems that are to do with the relative sizes of two amounts."

Worked Examples

1 **Eight** pencils cost **72p**. How much will **12** pencils cost?
Give your answer in **pounds**.

1) <u>Divide by 8</u> to find out how much
   <u>1 pencil</u> costs.

2) Then <u>multiply by 12</u> to find out
   how much <u>12 pencils</u> cost.

3) <u>Divide</u> by 100 to find the cost in <u>pounds</u>.

> 1 pencil costs 72p ÷ 8 = 9p
>
> 12 pencils cost 9p × 12 = 108p
>
> 108p ÷ 100 = £1.08

---

2 Write the **ratio** of **white** triangles
to **grey** triangles in this pattern.

1) <u>Count</u> the number of triangles of each colour.

2) So the ratio of white triangles to grey triangles is
   <u>3 to 4</u>. Replace 'to' with a ':' to write it as a <u>ratio</u>.

> 3 white triangles
> 4 grey triangles
>
> 3:4

---

3 A school has **5** science classrooms for every **6** maths classrooms. There are
10 science classrooms in the school. How many maths classrooms are there?

1) The ratio is <u>5 science classrooms</u>
   to <u>6 maths classrooms</u>.

2) **Work out** <u>how many lots</u> of
   <u>5 science classrooms</u> are in
   <u>10 science classrooms</u>.

3) This is <u>how many lots</u> of
   <u>6 maths classrooms</u> there are.

4) <u>Multiply</u> 6 by the number of lots to find
   the <u>number of maths classrooms</u>.

> 5:6
>
> 10 = 2 × 5
> 10 science classrooms
> = 2 lots of 5 science classrooms
>
> There are 2 lots of
> 6 maths classrooms.
>
> 2 × 6 = 12 maths classrooms

I get one telling-off for every six biscuits I eat...

The trick with ratios is to work out what one number in the ratio has been multiplied
by — then you can just multiply the other number in the ratio by the same amount.

Ratio and Proportion

Proportions Compare a Part to the Whole Thing

Look at this pattern. You could say that "In every 3 circles there are 2 white circles and 1 blue circle."
The <u>proportion</u> of white circles is <u>2 in every 3</u>.
The <u>proportion</u> of blue circles is <u>1 in every 3</u>.

> Proportions are really another way of writing fractions.
> The proportion "1 in every 3" is the same as the fraction $\frac{1}{3}$.

EXAMPLE: In my scarf collection, 5 in every 8 scarves are <u>striped</u>. I have 48 scarves in my collection. How many are striped?

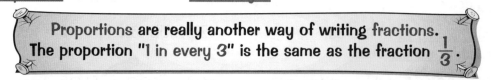

There are <u>5 striped scarves</u> in every <u>8</u>, so we need to know <u>how many 8s</u> there are in 48: $48 \div 8 = 6$.
So there are <u>6 lots</u> of <u>8 scarves</u> in the scarf collection.
So there must be <u>6 lots</u> of <u>5 striped scarves</u>. $6 \times 5 = \underline{30 \text{ striped scarves}}$.

You can use <u>proportions</u> in <u>recipes</u>...

EXAMPLE: A recipe for 4 people uses <u>5 oranges</u> and <u>3 socks</u>.

a) Rachel puts <u>12 socks</u> in. How many oranges does she need?
12 socks is <u>4 times</u> as many socks as in the recipe.
So she needs <u>4 times</u> as many oranges too. $4 \times 5 = \underline{20 \text{ oranges}}$.

b) How many socks and oranges would she need for <u>8 people</u>?
She needs <u>2 times</u> as many ingredients for 8 people as she does for 4.
So she will need $2 \times 5 = \underline{10 \text{ oranges}}$ and $2 \times 3 = \underline{6 \text{ socks}}$.

Sometimes Things are Shared Unequally

EXAMPLE: Joe eats <u>4 slices</u> of pie <u>for every 1</u> that Alison eats.

Another way to say this is:
"They share the pie in the ratio <u>4:1</u>".

<u>This means that</u>:
There are $\underline{4 + 1 = 5}$ shares of pie in total.
Alison gets 1 share and Joe gets 4 shares.

So Alison has $\frac{1}{5}$ of the total number of slices and Joe has $\frac{4}{5}$ of the total number.

If Alison has <u>3 slices</u> of pie, Joe has <u>four times</u> as many, so he has <u>12 slices</u>.
If Joe has <u>16 slices</u> of pie, Alison has <u>a quarter</u> of that amount, so she has <u>4 slices</u>.

Alison's share

Joe's share

"I can work out how to share things unequally."

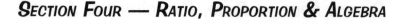

Worked Examples

1 Trevor owns **18** hats. **2 in every 3** of his hats are red.
How many red hats does Trevor own?

1) **Work out how many lots of <u>3 hats</u> are in <u>18 hats</u>.**

2) This is <u>how many lots</u> of <u>2 red hats</u> Trevor owns.

3) <u>Multiply</u> to find the number of red hats.

$18 = 6 \times 3$
18 hats = 6 lots of 3 hats

Trevor owns 6 lots of 2 red hats

$6 \times 2 = 12$ red hats

---

2 A recipe for **5 flapjacks** uses **200 g** of oats and **100 g** of sugar.
How much of each ingredient would be needed to make **15 flapjacks**?

1) **Work out how many lots of <u>5 flapjacks</u> are in <u>15 flapjacks</u>.**

2) This is <u>how many lots</u> of 200 g of oats and 100 g of sugar are needed.

3) <u>Multiply each ingredient</u> by this amount.

$15 = 3 \times 5$
15 flapjacks = 3 lots of 5 flapjacks

3 lots of 200 g of oats and
3 lots of 100 g of sugar are needed.

200 g $\times$ 3 = 600 g oats
100 g $\times$ 3 = 300 g sugar

---

3 Yasmin and Michael are sharing a box of **27 chocolates** in the ratio **5 : 4**.
How many chocolates does Yasmin get?

1) Yasmin gets <u>5 shares</u> and Michael gets <u>4 shares</u>, so there are <u>9 shares</u> in total.

2) <u>Divide 27 by 9</u> to find the number of chocolates in <u>one share</u>.

3) <u>Multiply this by 5</u> to find how many chocolates Yasmin gets.

5 + 4 = 9 shares in total

1 share = 27 ÷ 9 = 3 chocolates

Yasmin gets 5 × 3 = 15 chocolates

I always share my pizza in the ratio 10 : 1...

Once you've shared something in a ratio, adding up all the shares should get you back to the total in the question. If it doesn't, you know something's gone wrong.

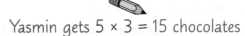

Percentage Problems

Finding Percentages of Amounts

Finding a percentage of an amount isn't too bad.
That's because...

$$10\% = \frac{10}{100} = \frac{1}{10}$$ ...and to find a tenth of
something, you just <u>divide by 10</u>.

So to <u>find 10% of something</u>, just <u>divide it by 10</u>.

EXAMPLE: What is 10% of 350 kg?

ANSWER: 10% of 350 = 350 ÷ 10 = <u>35 kg</u>

Finding <u>50%</u> is easy too.
50% is just a <u>half</u>.
For example, 50% of £80
is 80 ÷ 2 = £40.

If you can find <u>10%</u>, it's easy to find <u>20%</u> or <u>30%</u>.
(Just find 10% then <u>multiply</u> it by 2 or 3...)

You can also use 10% to find 5% or 15%.

EXAMPLE: Rose buys 700 g of cheese. She uses <u>5%</u> of the cheese
in her lunch. How many grams of cheese does she use?

Find <u>10%</u> of 700 g. Use that to find <u>5%</u> of 700 g.

<u>10% of 700 g</u> = 700 g ÷ 10
= <u>70 g</u>

5% is just
<u>half of 10%</u>

<u>5% of 700 g</u> = 70 g ÷ 2
= <u>35 g</u>

So Rose uses <u>35 g</u> of
cheese in her lunch.

Writing a Number as a Percentage of Another

To write <u>one number</u> as a <u>percentage of another number</u>,
write it as a <u>fraction</u> and then <u>convert to a percentage</u>.

EXAMPLE: There are <u>12 girls</u> and <u>8 boys</u> in a choir.
What <u>percentage</u> of the choir are <u>girls</u>?

First write the <u>total</u> number
of people in the choir as the
<u>denominator</u> of the fraction.

$$12 + 8 = 20 \longrightarrow \overline{20}$$

Then write the <u>number of girls</u> as the <u>numerator</u>.
Convert the fraction into a <u>percentage</u> (see page 46).

$$\frac{12}{20} \overset{\times 5}{=} \frac{60}{100} = \underline{60\%}$$
$$\times 5$$

"I can find a percentage of an amount."

Worked Examples

---

1 Victoria eats **40%** of a **150 g** chocolate bar.
How many **grams** of chocolate has she eaten?

1) Divide by 10 to find <u>10%</u> of 150 g.

2) <u>Multiply this by 4</u> to find 40%.

150 g ÷ 10 = 15 g

15 g × 4 = 60 g

 Victoria has eaten
60 g of chocolate.

---

2 Solomon has **£300**. He spends **15%** of his money on a new jacket.
What was the **price** of the jacket?

£300 ÷ 10 = £30

£30 ÷ 2 = £15

£30 + £15 = £45

 The price of the jacket was £45.

1) Divide by 10 to find <u>10%</u> of £300.

2) <u>Divide this by 2</u> to find 5%.

3) <u>Add together</u> the amounts to find 15%.

---

3 A car garage has **50 cars**. **15** of the cars are broken.
What **percentage** of the cars **aren't** broken?

1) <u>Subtract 15 from 50</u> to find the number of cars that <u>aren't broken</u>.

2) Write the number of cars that <u>aren't broken</u> as the numerator and the <u>total</u> number of cars as the denominator.

3) Make an <u>equivalent fraction</u> with <u>100</u> as the denominator.

4) The <u>numerator</u> is the percentage of cars that <u>aren't broken</u>.

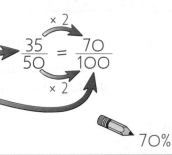

50 cars − 15 cars = 35 cars

$$\frac{35}{50} = \frac{70}{100}$$

× 2

70%

I bet you enjoy 100% of maths...

To convert a fraction to a percentage, you need to make the bottom 100 by multiplying or dividing. Then do the same to the top, and that's the percentage.

Formulas

A Formula *is* Used to Work Out an Amount

A formula tells you how to work out <u>one quantity</u> when you know a <u>different</u> quantity.

number of legs
= 4 × number of dogs

This formula is for working out <u>how many legs</u> a group of dogs has altogether.

EXAMPLE:

How <u>many</u> legs do <u>5 dogs</u> have altogether?

Substitute the <u>number of dogs</u> (5) into the formula:

number of legs = 4 × number of dogs
= 4 × 5
= <u>20 legs altogether</u>

EXAMPLE:

The formula for the <u>area</u> of a <u>parallelogram</u> is:

Area = Base × Height

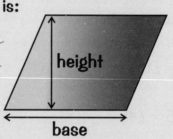

height

base

Find the area of a parallelogram where the base = 7 cm and the height = 4 cm.

1) Write out the <u>formula</u>.

2) Write it <u>again</u> underneath but with <u>numbers</u> in place of the words.

Area = Base × Height

Area = 7 × 4

Area = <u>28 cm²</u>

Don't forget — the answer might need a <u>unit of measurement</u>.

You Can *Write Your Own* Formula

This isn't as hard as it sounds. Just think about what you'd do if it were all numbers.

EXAMPLE: Garlic-flavoured cupcakes cost <u>63p each</u>. Write a formula so that you can calculate the <u>total cost</u> of buying any <u>number of cupcakes</u>.

Put what you want to work out before the "=" sign...

...then the calculation you'd do if it were numbers after it.

Total Cost = Number of cupcakes × 63p

"I can use formulas written in words."

Worked Examples

1 The formula for the number of chocolate chips in any number of cookies is: **Number of chocolate chips = 9 × Number of cookies**. How many chocolate chips would there be in **6 cookies**?

1) Write down the <u>formula</u> for the number of chocolate chips.
2) Do the calculation with <u>6</u> as the number of cookies.

> Number of chocolate chips
> = 9 × Number of cookies
> Number of chocolate chips = 9 × 6 = 54

2 The area of a kite is given by **Area = Height × Width × $\frac{1}{2}$**. Work out the area of a kite where **height = 3 cm** and **width = 6 cm**.

> Area = Height × Width × $\frac{1}{2}$
>
> Area = 3 × 6 × $\frac{1}{2}$
>
> Area = 18 × $\frac{1}{2}$ = 18 ÷ 2 = 9 cm²

1) Write down the <u>formula</u> for the area.
2) Write it again underneath with <u>height = 3</u> and <u>width = 6</u>.
3) Do the calculation in <u>stages</u>. First multiply <u>3 by 6</u>. Then multiply the answer by a <u>half</u>.
4) Don't forget the <u>units</u>.

3 Zainab has **3 times** as many T-shirts as jumpers. Write a formula for working out the number of **T-shirts** she has.

1) Write what you want to find <u>before</u> the '=' sign.

Number of T-shirts = 3 × Number of jumpers

2) The number of T-shirts is <u>3 times</u> the number of jumpers.

4 George can make **7 cups** of coffee from **one kettle** of water. Write a formula for the number of cups he can make from any number of kettles of water.

1) Write what you want to find <u>before</u> the '=' sign.
2) On the other side, write the <u>calculation</u> you would do if it were numbers.

> Number of cups of coffee = 7 × Number of kettles

If only there were a formula for a great joke...

It's really important that you remember units when you use a formula to calculate something. If a formula calculates a measurement, then you definitely need them.

Missing Number Problems

Symbols Can Stand For Missing Numbers

You can use a <u>symbol</u> to stand in for a number you don't know.

EXAMPLE: Claire <u>triples</u> her age and <u>adds six</u> to get 105. How old is she?

ANSWER: ◯ = Claire's age.

Remember to say what your symbol stands for.

Claire tripled her age, then <u>added 6</u> to get 105. So work backwards:
<u>105 – 6</u> must be <u>triple</u> Claire's age.

105 – 6 = 99
3 × ◯ = 99
So ◯ = 99 ÷ 3 = <u>33</u>

◯ is being multiplied by 3, so divide both sides by 3 to get ◯ on its own.

Letters Are Often Used Instead Of Symbols

You can also use a <u>letter</u> to stand for a number that you don't know. It's quicker and easier than drawing a symbol every time.

If y is the unknown number then:

$y + 5$ means you are <u>adding 5</u> to it.
$y - 3$ means you are <u>subtracting 3</u> from it.
$6y$ means you are <u>multiplying it by 6</u> ($6 \times y$).

EXAMPLE: Jane has <u>32</u> eggs. Jane has <u>4 times</u> as many as Gary. How many eggs does Gary have?

The number of eggs Gary has is unknown. Call this y eggs. Jane has 32 eggs, which is $4 \times y$ (4 times as many as Gary).

So $4y = 32$
$y = 32 ÷ 4 = 8$
So Gary has <u>8 eggs</u>.

Divide both sides by 4 to get y on its own.

Problems Can Have Two Missing Numbers

EXAMPLE: Alan is told that <u>A × B = 30</u>, where A and B are <u>whole numbers</u>. Write down 3 possible <u>pairs of values</u> for A and B.

Try different numbers for A, and work out what B would need to be to give 30.

Try A = 1. 1 × 30 = 30, so B = 30.

Try A = 2. 2 × 15 = 30, so B = 15.

Try A = 3. 3 × 10 = 30, so B = 10. That's 3 possible pairs, so stop there.

"I can solve missing number problems using symbols and letters. I can find pairs of numbers to solve problems with two unknowns."

Worked Examples

1 Steve thinks of a number. He **doubles** it and **subtracts 8** to get **100**. What number did he think of?

1) <u>Pick a letter</u> to stand for Steve's number.

2) Work backwards — so <u>add 8</u> first.

3) So Steve's number <u>multiplied by 2</u> is **108**.

4) <u>Divide 108 by 2</u> to give Steve's number.

n = Steve's number

$100 + 8 = 108$

$2 \times n = 108$

$n = 108 \div 2 = 54$

---

2 Chris is **45 years old**. Chris is **5 times older** than Angela. How old is Angela?

1) <u>Pick a letter</u> to stand for Angela's age.

2) Chris's age is <u>5 times</u> Angela's age.

3) <u>Divide both sides by 5</u> to find Angela's age.

A = Angela's age

$5A = 45$

$A = 45 \div 5 = 9$

9 years old

---

3 4G + H = 15
Find **3 possible pairs** of values for G and H.

1) <u>Try different values for G</u>, then work out what <u>H</u> would need to be to <u>make 15</u>.

If G = 1: 4G = 4, so 4 + H = 15 and H = 11
If G = 2: 4G = 8, so 8 + H = 15 and H = 7
If G = 3: 4G = 12, so 12 + H = 15 and H = 3

 Three possible pairs are:
G = 1, H = 11
G = 2, H = 7
G = 3, H = 3

2) After you've found <u>3 pairs</u> of values for G and H, stop. <u>Write down</u> the pairs.

Symbols and letters — I thought this was maths...

You can check your answer to missing number problems. Just put your answer back into the calculation in the question to see if you get the number you expect.

Practice Questions

1   Hitesh buys eight T-shirts for £56. Each T-shirt is the same price.

What is the cost of one T-shirt?

2   A zoo has a special offer on tickets. The zoo is offering 1 free ticket for every six tickets bought.

Ellie buys 30 tickets. How many free tickets does she get?

3   Brad is organising a picnic. For every 5 people at the picnic he plans to bring 15 sandwiches and 10 sausage rolls.

He invites 15 people to his picnic.
How many sandwiches and sausage rolls should he bring?

4   Monisha and Vicky share the money they make on their market stall in the ratio 6:5.

One day, they make £66. How much money does each of them get?

5   Sarah and Rahul have a car boot sale.
For every 2 items Rahul sold, Sarah sold 3.

a)   Write this as a ratio.

b)   If Rahul sold 18 items, how many did Sarah sell?

6   Work out these percentages.

a)   10% of £160

b)   15% of 120 kg

c)   30% of 70 cm

7   A running club has 18 members aged 30 or above, and 7 members aged under 30.

What percentage of their members are under 30?

Practice Questions

8   Lauren did a maths quiz with 20 questions.
She got four of the questions wrong.

     What percentage of the questions did she get right?

9   The area of a rhombus is given by: Area = First Diagonal × Second Diagonal × $\frac{1}{2}$

     Find the area of a rhombus
where the first diagonal = 6 cm
and the second diagonal = 8 cm.

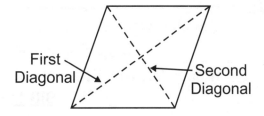

First Diagonal   Second Diagonal

10   A shop sells 6 times as many bananas as apples.

     Write down a formula for the number of bananas the shop sells.

11   A holiday provider charges a booking fee
of £15 per person when booking a holiday.

     Write a formula to work out the total booking fee for any number of people.

12   Find the value of the symbols in the calculations below.

     a) $7 + \bigstar = 104$ b) $\square - 15 = 37$

     c) $8 \times \bigcirc = 96$ d) $\triangle \div 12 = 7$

13   Elliot has £48. He has 8 times as much money as Ryan.

     How much money does Ryan have?

14   Sam is told that 3M + N = 17.

     Find 4 possible pairs of values for M and N.

Units and Conversions

Sometimes You Need to Convert Units

You can change from one unit to another. They can be <u>metric</u> or <u>imperial</u> units.

METRIC		IMPERIAL
1 cm = 10 mm	1 kg = 1000 g	1 ft = 12 in
1 m = 100 cm	1 litre = 1000 ml	1 lb = 16 oz
1 km = 1000 m		1 gallon = 8 pints

'oz' means 'ounces' and 'lbs' means 'pounds'.

If you start with small units, a conversion gives <u>fewer</u> BIGGER units.
To go from <u>small to BIG</u> units, <u>DIVIDE</u>.

If you start with BIG units, a conversion gives <u>more</u> smaller units.
To go from <u>BIG to small</u> units, <u>MULTIPLY</u>.

EXAMPLE: Ryan cycles <u>3654 m</u> to school. Heather cycles <u>300 m</u> further.
How far does Heather cycle to school in <u>kilometres</u>?

Heather travels 3654 + 300 = <u>3954 m</u>.
But you need to give your answer in <u>kilometres</u>...

There are 1000 m in 1 km, so the <u>conversion factor</u> is <u>1000</u>.
Metres are SMALLER than km, so <u>divide by 1000</u>.

3954 m ÷ 1000
= <u>3.954 km</u>

You Can Convert Between Metric and Imperial

You can convert <u>imperial units</u> to <u>metric units</u>, or the other way round.
For example, you could change a distance in <u>feet</u> to a distance in <u>metres</u>.

1 metre ≈ 3 feet	5 centimetres ≈ 2 inches
1 kilogram ≈ 2 pounds	8 kilometres ≈ 5 miles
1 litre ≈ 2 pints	100 grams ≈ 4 ounces

The sign '≈' means 'is <u>about equal</u> to'. These conversions aren't exact but it's fine to use them for rough calculations.

EXAMPLE: Henry gets covered in 8 litres of slime.
How many pints is this?

① Find the <u>conversion factor</u> you need: <u>1 litre ≈ 2 pints</u>.

② Every 1 litre is 2 pints, so you will have twice as many pints as litres. So you need to <u>multiply by 2</u>.

8 × 2 = 16

③ Henry gets covered in about <u>16 pints</u> of slime.

"I can convert between units for measurements of length, mass and volume."

Worked Examples

(1) Convert **4.27 kg** into **grams**.

1 kg = 1000 g

4.27 × 1000 = 4270

 4270 g

1) There are <u>1000 g</u> in <u>1 kg</u>, so the conversion factor is <u>1000</u>.

2) You're going from a <u>big unit</u> to a <u>small unit</u>, so <u>multiply</u> by the conversion factor.

(2) **1 ft = 12 inches**. Catherine is **58 inches** tall. How tall is she in **feet** and **inches**?

1 ft = 12 inches

58 ÷ 12 = 4 r 10

 Catherine is 4 ft 10 in tall.

1) There are <u>12 inches</u> in <u>1 ft</u>, so the conversion factor is <u>12</u>.

2) You're going from a <u>small unit</u> to a <u>big unit</u>, so <u>divide</u> by the conversion factor.

3) The <u>remainder</u> is the number of inches.

(3) Selby weighed **3.5 kg** when he was born. Given that **1 kg ≈ 2 lbs**, approximately how much did Selby weigh in pounds?

1) There are about <u>2 lbs</u> in <u>1 kg</u>, so the conversion factor is <u>2</u>.

2) You're going from a <u>big unit</u> to a <u>small unit</u>, so <u>multiply</u> by the conversion factor.

1 kg ≈ 2 lbs   3.5 × 2 = 7

 Selby weighed about 7 lbs.

(4) Steven's sunflower grew **6 inches** in one month. Given that **5cm ≈ 2 in**, approximately how many **cm** did Steven's sunflower grow?

1) There are about <u>5 cm</u> in <u>2 in</u>.

2) 6 inches is <u>3 lots</u> of 2 inches. That's equal to about <u>3 lots</u> of 5 cm.

5 cm ≈ 2 in   3 × 5 = 15

 It grew about 15 cm.

The Conversion Factor — TV's newest gameshow...

For metric units, the conversion factors are always 10, 100 or 1000 which are nice and easy to work with. Imperial units have more awkward conversion factors like 16.

Calculating with Measures

Some Problems Could Involve Converting Time

You need to know these time conversions:

> 1 minute = 60 seconds
> 1 hour = 60 minutes
> 1 day = 24 hours
>
> 1 week = 7 days
> 1 year = 365 days

A leap year has 366 days.

EXAMPLE: It took Pat 195 minutes to paint a wall.
How long is this in hours and minutes?

There are 60 minutes in an hour, so you need to work out 195 ÷ 60.
60 × 3 = 180, so 195 ÷ 60 = 3 remainder 15.

This means 3 hours and 15 minutes.

So it took Pat 3 hours and 15 minutes to paint the wall.

Choose the Easiest Way to Do Things

EXAMPLE: Sylvia has a necklace that is 60 cm long.
It is made from beads which are 12 mm long.
How many beads are there in Sylvia's necklace?

You have to find out how many times 12 mm goes into 60 cm.

Change the 60 cm into mm first. → 60 × 10 = 600 mm

So now the problem is 'How many 12s go into 600?'

Make sure the units match.

You have to find out how many times 12 mm goes into 600 mm. → 600 ÷ 12 = 50 beads

EXAMPLE: A bag of Oscar the rabbit's favourite food costs £8.50.
His least favourite food costs 86 p less.
How much does his least favourite food cost?

You have to take away 86 pence from £8.50.
Change £8.50 into pence first. ✎ 8.5 × 100 = 850 pence
Now subtract. ✎ 850 − 86 = 764 pence.

**Convert your answer back to £:
764 ÷ 100
= £7.64**

"I can solve problems that involve converting between units."

Worked Examples

(1) David goes on holiday for **2 days**. How many **minutes** is this?

1) Start by converting <u>days</u> into <u>hours</u>. There are **24** hours in a day, so <u>multiply</u> by <u>24</u>.

2) Now convert <u>hours</u> into <u>minutes</u>. There are **60** minutes in an hour, so <u>multiply</u> by <u>60</u>.

$$2 \times 24 = 48 \text{ hours}$$

```
     4 8
   × 6 0
   -----
     0 0
   2 8,8 0
   -----
   2 8 8 0
```
2880 minutes

(2) Kim has **£23.50**. She buys a bottle of water for **43p** and a bag of crisps for **50p**. How much money does she have left now?

$$43 + 50 = 93p$$

$$£23.50 \times 100 = 2350p$$

```
   2 3 5 0
 -     9 3
   -------
   2 2 5 7
```

$$2257 \div 100 = 22.57$$
£22.57

1) Add together <u>43p</u> and <u>50p</u>.

2) Convert <u>£23.50</u> into <u>pence</u>. £1 = 100p, so <u>multiply</u> by <u>100</u>.

3) Now <u>subtract</u> 93p from 2350p.

4) Convert your answer back to pounds — <u>divide</u> by <u>100</u>.

(3) Kerry uses **35 ml** of milk to make one milk ice lolly. She has a **0.7 litre** bottle of milk. How many milk ice lollies can she make?

1) Convert 0.7 litres into ml. There are 1000 ml in 1 litre, so multiply by <u>1000</u>.

2) Now divide 700 by 35. (70 ÷ 35 = 2, so 70<u>0</u> ÷ 35 = 2<u>0</u>).

$$0.7 \times 1000 = 700 \text{ ml}$$

$$700 \div 35 = 20$$

Kerry can make 20 ice lollies

A leap year — a year with lots of jumping...

Converting units is just multiplying and dividing — so nothing too scary here. Make sure you get the units to match first before you do any other calculations.

Perimeter

Finding the Perimeters of Shapes

1) To find a perimeter, just add up the lengths of all the sides.
2) Make sure you get all the sides.
   It's best to mark one vertex with a blob or cross...
3) ...then work your way around the shape, adding as you go.

EXAMPLE: Trang has an unusually shaped slice of pizza.
Find its perimeter.

You've been given the lengths of
all the sides apart from this one...

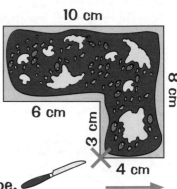

10 cm

8 cm

6 cm

3 cm

4 cm

The 'missing' side plus 3 cm must be the same
length as the side opposite, which is 8 cm.
So the missing side must be 8 cm – 3 cm = 5 cm.

Put a big cross on one vertex, then work around the shape.
The perimeter is: 4 + 8 + 10 + 5 + 6 + 3 = **36 cm**.

You Might Have to Measure some Sides

EXAMPLE: This shape is made from 3 equilateral triangles. Find its perimeter.

Luckily you don't have to measure all of the sides...
They're equilateral triangles so all the sides are the same length.

Measure one side. One side is 2 cm long.
The perimeter is made up of all 3 sides from each triangle.
There are three triangles, so 3 × 3 = 9 sides altogether.

So the perimeter = 9 × 2 cm = **18 cm**.

There Can Be More Than One Missing Length

EXAMPLE: Find the perimeter of this swimming pool.

Work out the missing sides **A** and **B**.

8 m

A   4 m

4 m

10 m

B

4 m

6 m

1 The vertical length of the pool is 10 m.
A + 4 m + 4 m = 10 m, so **A** = **2 m**

2 The horizontal length of the pool is 8 m + 4 m = 12 m.
6 m + B = 12 m, so **B** = **6 m**

So the perimeter is 10 + 8 + 2 + 4 + 4 + 6 + 4 + 6 = **44 m**.

"I can measure and calculate
the perimeters of shapes."

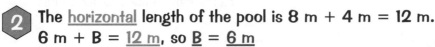

Worked Examples

1 Calculate the perimeter of a **regular octagon** with side lengths of **6 cm**.

1) A regular octagon has <u>eight equal sides</u>...

2) ...so <u>multiply</u> **6** by **8**.

$8 \times 6 = 48$

 48 cm

2 This shape is made from **three regular pentagons**.
Find the perimeter of the shape in **mm**.

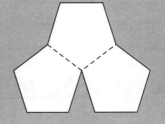

1) <u>Measure</u> one side of the shape.

2) <u>Count</u> how many sides there are.

3) Since the shape is made up of <u>regular</u> pentagons, each side will be the <u>same</u> length. So <u>multiply</u> the <u>length</u> of each side by the <u>number</u> of sides.

One side = 12 mm

There are 11 sides.

$12 \times 11 = 132$

132 mm

3 Here's a diagram of Binh's garden.
Work out the **perimeter** of his garden.

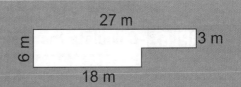

27 m
3 m
6 m
18 m

$27 \text{ m} - 18 \text{ m} = 9 \text{ m}$

$6 \text{ m} - 3 \text{ m} = 3 \text{ m}$

$6 + 27 + 3 + 9 + 3 + 18 = 66$

66 m

1) Find the missing <u>horizontal</u> length.
The horizontal length of the garden is <u>27 m</u>.
So the missing length will be <u>27 m – 18 m</u>.

2) Now find the missing <u>vertical</u> length.
The vertical length of the garden is <u>6 m</u>.
So the missing length will be <u>6 m – 3 m</u>.

3) Add up all the side lengths to find the <u>perimeter</u>.

All this perimeter stuff is starting to add up...

Don't panic if some of the side lengths are missing when you're asked to find the perimeter. Doing a little bit of detective work will give you the answer...

Area

You Can Estimate Area by Counting Squares

You can find areas by counting <u>how many squares</u> or <u>half-squares</u> are covered on a grid.

But not all shapes fit neatly into whole or half squares. You can <u>estimate</u> these areas by counting <u>how many squares</u> are <u>more than half covered</u>.

EXAMPLE:

<u>2</u> squares are more than half covered by this snot-coloured goo. So its area is about <u>2 cm²</u>.

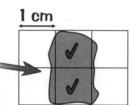

1 cm

Each square has sides 1 cm long, so the units are <u>square centimetres</u>, or <u>cm²</u>.

Area of Squares and Rectangles — Just Multiply

There's a quick way of working out the <u>areas</u> of <u>squares</u> and <u>rectangles</u> to save you the hassle of counting all the squares.

Count how many squares <u>long</u> the shape is and how many squares <u>wide</u> it is. Then <u>multiply</u> these numbers together.

→ Area = Length × Width

EXAMPLE: Work out the area of this rectangle.
There are <u>5 rows</u> of 8 squares.
So the area is 5 × 8 = <u>40 cm²</u>

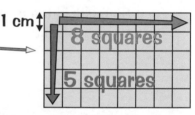

1 cm
8 squares
5 squares

EXAMPLE: Calculate the area of a rectangle measuring 6 m by 9 m.

Just <u>multiply</u> the sides together. → Area = 6 × 9 = <u>54 m²</u>

Use the Area to Find Missing Lengths

Sometimes there's a <u>side length</u> missing. If you know the <u>area</u> of a square or rectangle, you can use <u>area = length × width</u> to work out a missing <u>side</u>.

EXAMPLE: A rectangle has a width of <u>4 cm</u> and an area of <u>32 cm²</u>.
What is its length?

Area = length × width, so 32 = length × 4

→ 32 ÷ 4 = 8... →

...so the rectangle has a length of <u>8 cm</u>.

"I can measure and calculate the areas of shapes."

Worked Examples

1   Find the **area** of the shaded shape on this grid.   1 cm

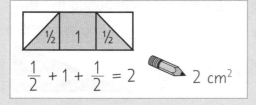

$\frac{1}{2} + 1 + \frac{1}{2} = 2$ 2 cm²

1) Count how many squares are covered.

2) Don't forget the <u>units</u>.

---

2   **Estimate** the **area** of the shaded part shown on this grid.   1 cm

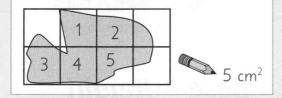

5 cm²

1) Count how many squares are <u>more than half covered</u>.

2) Don't forget the <u>units</u>.

---

3   Calculate the **area** of this rectangle.

5 cm   12 cm

length × width

12 × 5 = 60   60 cm²

1) The length of the rectangle is <u>12 cm</u>. The width of the rectangle is <u>5 cm</u>.

2) Use length × width to find the area. Don't forget the <u>units</u>.

---

4   Liann's vegetable patch is a rectangle with an area of **72 m²**. It has a length of 6 m. What is its width?

1) Length × width = area, so <u>fill in</u> the numbers you're given in the question.

2) <u>Divide</u> the <u>area</u> by the <u>length</u> to find the width.

3) So the vegetable patch has a width of <u>12 m</u>.

Area = length × width

72 = 6 × width

72 ÷ 6 = 12

12 m

I searched the whole area for the missing length...

Sometimes you might have to count squares or measure sides to find the area. Other times, there might be a side missing and you have to work it out from the area.

Areas of Triangles and Parallelograms

A Triangle is Half a Rectangle

There's a rule you can use to work out the area of a triangle.
A right-angled triangle covers <u>half</u> the area of the <u>rectangle</u> that surrounds it, so...

It works for all triangles, but you must use the <u>vertical</u> height.

Area of triangle = $\frac{1}{2}$ × Base × Height

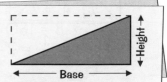

EXAMPLE: Find the area of this triangle.

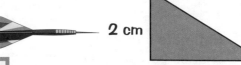

The base is <u>4 cm</u> and the height is <u>2 cm</u>.
Area = $\frac{1}{2}$ × 4 × 2 = <u>4 cm²</u>

Multiplying by a half is the same as dividing by 2.

Area of a Parallelogram = Base × Height

A parallelogram is like a rectangle that's been <u>pushed over</u>.
To find the <u>area</u> of a <u>parallelogram</u>, you can use the rule:

Area of Parallelogram = Base × Height

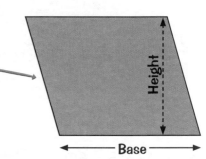

EXAMPLES:

a) Find the area of this parallelogram.

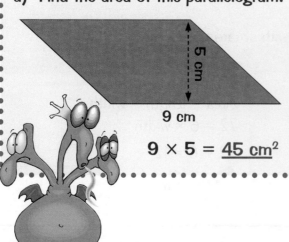

9 cm

5 cm

9 × 5 = <u>45 cm²</u>

b) Lee has a parallelogram-shaped rug. Find its area.

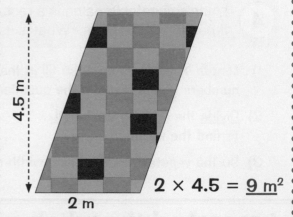

4.5 m

2 m

2 × 4.5 = <u>9 m²</u>

"I can calculate the area of a triangle.
I can calculate the area of a parallelogram."

Worked Examples

1 Find the area of a parallelogram which has a base of **20 cm** and a height of **8 cm**.

base × height

20 × 8 = 160

 160 cm²

1) The area of a parallelogram is <u>base × height</u>.

2) Replace 'base' with <u>20</u> and 'height' with <u>8</u>...

3) ...then do the multiplication.
Don't forget the <u>units</u>.

---

2 Calculate the **area** of this triangle.

3 cm

6 cm

$\frac{1}{2}$ × base × height

$\frac{1}{2}$ × 6 × 3 = 9   9 cm²

1) The base of the triangle is <u>6 cm</u>.
The height of the triangle is <u>3 cm</u>.

2) Use $\frac{1}{2}$ × base × height to find the area of the triangle.

---

3 Here's a plan of Ryan's garden. He has a **rectangular** lawn and a **triangular** pond. Find the area of his whole garden.

3 m   4 m

7 m

1) Find the <u>area</u> of the <u>rectangle</u> first.

2) Now calculate the <u>area</u> of the <u>triangle</u>.

3) Add together to find the <u>total</u> area.

4) Don't forget the <u>units</u>.

area of rectangle: 7 × 4 = 28 m²

area of triangle: $\frac{1}{2}$ × 4 × 3 = 6 m²

total area = 28 + 6 = 34

 34 m²

The rectangle hated being pushed over...

You'll need to know the base and the height to find out the area of both a triangle and a parallelogram. Just don't forget about that sneaky half in the area of a triangle.

Volume

You Can Count Cubes for All Sorts of Shapes

The volume of a shape is the <u>amount of space</u> it takes up.

Say you've got a <u>3D shape</u> made up of <u>cubes</u> with sides of <u>1 cm</u>...

EXAMPLE: Find the volume of this 3D shape.

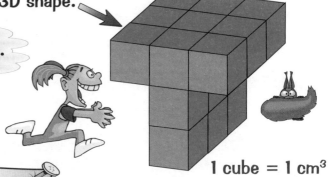

The T shape is made up of <u>5 cubes</u>.

It's **3 cubes deep**, so do 5 × 3 = <u>15 cubes</u>.

1 cube = 1 cm³

Each cube has a volume of 1 cm³. So 15 cubes have a volume of <u>15 cm³</u>.

There's a Formula for Calculating Volume

There's a quicker way of working out the volume of cubes and cuboids by measuring the <u>lengths</u> of the <u>sides</u>:

It's the same formula for cubes too.

> **Volume of Cuboid = Length × Width × Height**
> **V = L × W × H**

EXAMPLE:

Find the <u>volume</u> of an ice cube with sides of <u>4 cm</u>.

Volume = Length × Width × Height

= 4 × 4 × 4 = <u>64 cm³</u>

EXAMPLE: Find the <u>volume</u> of this cuboid.

Volume = Length × Width × Height

= 12 × 5 × 10 = <u>600 cm³</u>

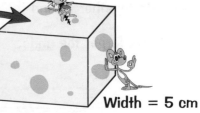

Height = 10 cm

Width = 5 cm

Length = 12 cm

"I can calculate the volumes of cubes and cuboids."

Worked Examples

1 Each cube has sides of **1 cm**. Find the **volume** of this shape.

1) Each cube has a volume of <u>1 cm³</u>.
   <u>Count</u> the number of cubes in the shape.

2) Multiply the <u>number of cubes</u> by the <u>volume</u>.

> 6 cubes
>
> 6 × 1 = 6   6 cm³

2 Find the volume of a cuboid with length **6 cm**, width **7 cm** and height **3 cm**.

1) **Find the volume of a cuboid by using the formula** <u>volume = length × width × height</u>.

2) **Replace 'length' with** <u>6</u>, **'width' with** <u>7</u> **and 'height' with** <u>3</u>. **Then** <u>multiply</u>.

> volume = length × width × height
>
> = 6 × 7 × 3 = 126   126 cm³

3 Imogen has some steps for her dolls' house. Work out the **volume** of the steps.

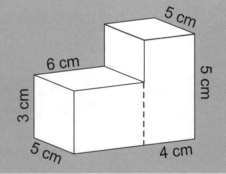

Volume of left-hand cuboid:
length × width × height
6 × 5 × 3 = <u>90 cm²</u>

Volume of right-hand cuboid:
length × width × height
4 × 5 × 5 = <u>100 cm²</u>

Total volume:
90 + 100 = 190 cm³

1) The block is made up of <u>two steps</u>.

2) Start by working out the <u>volume</u> of the <u>left-hand</u> cuboid. The length is <u>6 cm</u>, the width is <u>5 cm</u> and the height is <u>3 cm</u>.

3) Now work out the <u>volume</u> of the <u>right-hand</u> cuboid. The length is <u>4 cm</u>, the width is <u>5 cm</u> and the height is <u>5 cm</u>.

4) Add both the volumes together — don't forget the <u>units</u>.

Crank up the volume — this stuff is getting good...

You're on the last few pages of this section now — just in time to learn about finding the volume of shapes. Exciting stuff. Make sure you don't forget the units though...

Practice Questions

1   Given that 1 lb = 16 ounces, convert the following:

    a)   3 pounds into ounces.   b)   64 ounces into pounds.

2   Given that 5 cm ≈ 2 inches, convert the following:

    a)   15 centimetres into inches.   b)   20 inches into centimetres.

3   It takes Matilda 84 hours to cycle from Leamington to Paris.

    How long is this in days and hours?

4   Miss Honey has just milked her cow. She has collected
    3 litres of milk and pours it into bottles which can hold 500 ml.

    How many milk bottles does she fill?

5   Agatha buys two apps for her mobile phone.
    One costs £3.85 and the other costs 79p.

    How much does she spend on apps in total?

6   At the start of Year 6, Harry was 1.37 m tall.
    He grew 42 mm over the whole school year.

    How tall was he at the end of Year 6? Give your answer in centimetres.

7   Magnus makes a cake for his younger brother's birthday.

    Work out the perimeter of his cake.

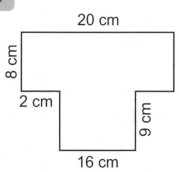

Practice Questions

8   Each side of Bruce's hexagonal patio is the same length. It has a perimeter of 18 m.

How long is each side of Bruce's patio?

9   Zinnia has discovered a new island. Here is her map.

Calculate the area of the island.

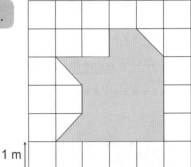

10   Calculate the areas of the following shapes:

1 m

a)   A square with sides of length 9 cm.

b)   A rectangle with length 7 m and width 6 m.

c)   A triangle with base 3 mm and height 8 mm.

d)   A parallelogram with base 4 cm and height 9 cm.

11   Lavendar makes a pattern from a parallelogram and two identical triangles.

Find the area of her pattern.

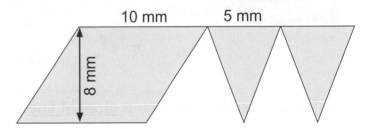

10 mm   5 mm

8 mm

12   A cuboid has a length of 3 cm, a width of 4 cm and a height of 6 cm.

Find the volume of the cuboid.

13   Michael has a wooden cuboid.
It has a length of 5 cm, a width of 2 cm and a volume of 100 cm^3.

What is the height of his cuboid?

Angles

Different Size Angles have Different Names

Angles are given different <u>names</u> according to how <u>big</u> they are:

If it's <u>less</u> than a $\frac{1}{4}$ turn, then it's an <u>ACUTE</u> angle.

If it's <u>exactly</u> a $\frac{1}{4}$ turn, then it's a <u>RIGHT</u> angle.

The little square shows that it's a right angle.

If it's between a $\frac{1}{4}$ and $\frac{1}{2}$ turn, then it's an <u>OBTUSE</u> angle.

If it's <u>more</u> than a $\frac{1}{2}$ turn, then it's a <u>REFLEX</u> angle.

Use Angle Sums to Work Out Missing Angles

The angles <u>around a point</u> (a full turn) add up to <u>360°</u>.

EXAMPLE: Find angle k.

150°
30°
75° k

$75° + 150° + 30° + k = 360°$
$255° + k = 360°$ so $k = 360° - 255° = \underline{105°}$

The angles that meet on a <u>straight line</u> (half a turn) add up to <u>180°</u>.

EXAMPLE: Find angle a.

80°
65° a

$65° + 80° + a = 180°$
$145° + a = 180°$ so $a = 180° - 145° = \underline{35°}$

The angles that meet at a <u>quarter turn</u> (a <u>right angle</u>) add up to <u>90°</u>.

EXAMPLE: Find angle z.

z
50°

$50° + z = 90°$
So $z = 90° - 50° = \underline{40°}$

"I know the sums of angles around a point, on a straight line and in a right angle."

Worked Examples

1 Fill in the table with the **name** of each **type** of angle.

1) The first angle is <u>between a quarter turn and a half turn</u>. It is an <u>obtuse</u> angle.

2) The second angle is <u>more</u> than a <u>half turn</u>. It is a <u>reflex</u> angle.

3) The third angle is <u>less</u> than a <u>quarter turn</u>. It is an <u>acute</u> angle.

4) The final angle is a <u>quarter turn</u>. It is a <u>right angle</u>.

Angle	Name
	Obtuse
	Reflex
	Acute
	Right angle

2 Joshua says that the size of **angle x** in this diagram is **65°**. **Explain** how you know he is **incorrect**.

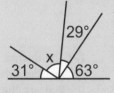

Work out the <u>sum</u> of the angles. They are on a <u>straight line</u> — they should add up to <u>180°</u>.

$31° + 29° + 63° + 65° = 188°$

Joshua is incorrect because the angles do not add up to 180°.

3 This circle has been divided into **6 equal pieces**. Work out the size of **angle a**.

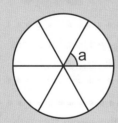

There are <u>360°</u> in the full turn around the centre of the circle. <u>Divide by 6</u> to find the size of angle a.

$360° ÷ 6 = 60°$

$a = 60°$

Awww — that's such a cute angle...

Right-angles aren't always labelled — so don't forget that the little square means it's a 90° angle. It's a quarter of a full turn, which means it's 360° ÷ 4. Good eh?

2D Shapes

Learn the Properties of These Shapes

<u>Regular polygons</u> have <u>equal length sides</u> and <u>equal angles</u>, such as...

pentagon
5 sides

hexagon
6 sides

heptagon
7 sides

octagon
8 sides

<u>Irregular polygons</u> have at least <u>1 side</u> or <u>angle</u> that's different in size.

<u>Quadrilaterals</u> are <u>four-sided</u> shapes:

SQUARE
4 equal sides.
Diagonals meet
at right angles.

 4 right angles.
2 pairs of parallel sides.

Parallel sides are the same distance apart and never meet.

RECTANGLE
2 pairs of
equal sides.

 **RHOMBUS**
4 sides of
equal length.

Opposite sides are parallel. Opposite angles are equal.

PARALLELOGRAM
Opposite sides are
the same length.

KITE
2 pairs of equal-length
sides. No parallel sides.
1 pair of equal angles

TRAPEZIUM
1 pair of
parallel sides.

 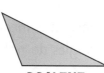 Matching arrows
show parallel sides.

There are Four Types of Triangle

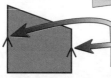

EQUILATERAL
3 equal sides,
3 equal angles

SCALENE
<u>All</u> sides and angles
are <u>different</u>

RIGHT ANGLED
1 <u>right angle</u>

ISOSCELES
2 equal sides,
2 equal angles

The dashes show the sides that are the same length.

Learn the Parts of a Circle

You need to know the different <u>parts of a circle</u>.

The distance from the <u>edge to the centre</u> of the circle is called the <u>radius</u>.

  circumference

The <u>outside edge</u> of a circle is called the <u>circumference</u>.

The distance <u>across the circle</u> through the centre is called the <u>diameter</u>.

"I know the properties of different shapes.
I can name the parts of a circle."

Worked Examples

1 What type of **triangle** is shown below?

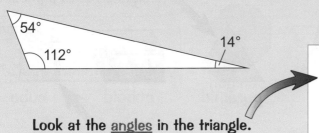

54°
112°
14°

Look at the angles in the triangle.

All of the angles are different.
None of the angles are right angles.

Scalene triangle

---

2 Draw lines to **match** each **shape** to the correct **name** and **description**.

1) The first shape is a regular pentagon.

2) The second shape is a kite.

3) The third shape is a trapezium.

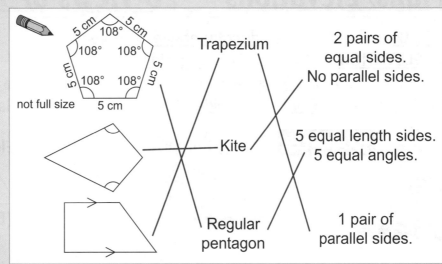

5 cm 5 cm
108°
108° 108°
5 cm 5 cm
108° 108°
5 cm
not full size

Trapezium

Kite

Regular pentagon

2 pairs of equal sides. No parallel sides.

5 equal length sides. 5 equal angles.

1 pair of parallel sides.

---

3 What is the **name** of this polygon?

95°
85°
125° 150°
85°

1) The shape has 5 sides — it is a pentagon.

2) Most of the angles are different — it is irregular.

Irregular pentagon

Phew — so many shapes, so little time...

Without looking at these pages, try writing down the names and properties of as many of these shapes as you can. I know it's confusing — but you need to know it.

3D Shapes

3D Shapes are Solid Shapes

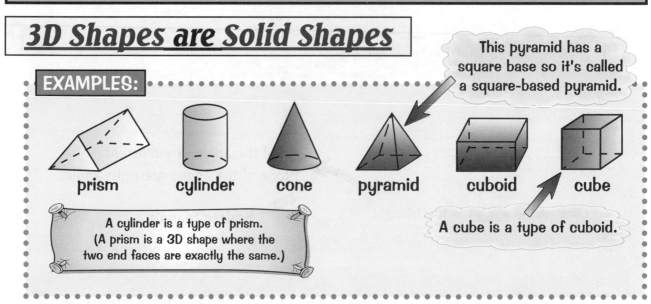

EXAMPLES:

prism   cylinder   cone   pyramid   cuboid   cube

This pyramid has a square base so it's called a square-based pyramid.

A cylinder is a type of prism. (A prism is a 3D shape where the two end faces are exactly the same.)

A cube is a type of cuboid.

Plans/Elevations — 2D Views of 3D Shapes

A <u>PLAN</u> is the view from <u>directly above</u> an object.

An <u>ELEVATION</u> is the view from <u>one side</u>.

Elevations might be <u>different</u> depending on whether you're looking from the <u>front</u> or the <u>side</u> (like in the triangular prism below).

Elevations are also called <u>projections</u>.

EXAMPLE: Triangular prism

Plan:

Elevation:

or

(front)   (side)

You Fold a Net to make a 3D Shape

The <u>shape of each face</u> on a 3D solid makes up part of the <u>solid's net</u>.

There's often <u>more than one net</u> you can use to make a 3D shape.

EXAMPLE: Cuboid

7 cm

4 cm

7 cm

11 cm

4 cm   4 cm

4 cm

11 cm

7 cm

All the faces are <u>rectangles</u>.

The net of a <u>prism</u> has two <u>end faces</u> that are the <u>same</u>. All the other faces are <u>rectangles</u>.

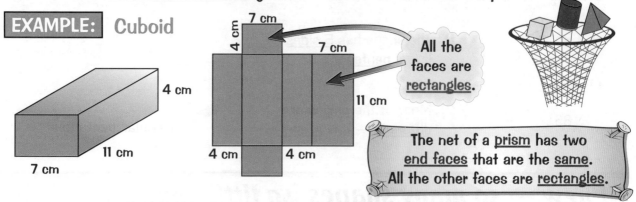

"I can recognise and describe 3D shapes.
I can draw nets of 3D shapes."

Worked Examples

(1) The **net** of a shape is drawn below. Name the **shape** the net makes.

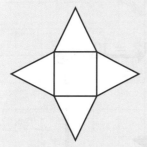

Square-based pyramid

The net has <u>one square face</u> and <u>four triangular faces</u>, so it's a <u>square-based pyramid</u>.

(2) Draw lines to match each shape to its **plan view**.

1) The first shape is a <u>triangle-based pyramid</u>. Its <u>plan view</u> is a <u>triangle</u> with the outlines of its other faces visible.

2) The second shape is a <u>cylinder</u>. Its <u>plan view</u> is a <u>circle</u>.

3) The third shape is a <u>cube</u>. Its <u>plan view</u> is a <u>square</u>.

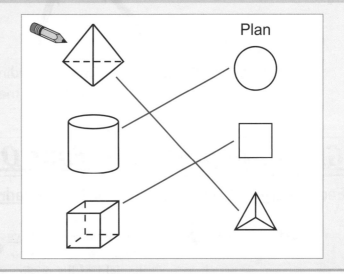

Plan

(3) Complete the drawing of this **net** of a **triangular prism**.

1) The net needs <u>2 triangular faces</u> and <u>3 rectangular faces</u>. Draw the missing <u>triangular face</u> on the <u>opposite</u> side of the rectangle to the other triangle. The triangles should be <u>identical</u>.

2) Draw the missing <u>rectangular face</u>. Its <u>length</u> should be the <u>same</u> as the <u>height</u> of the <u>triangles</u>.

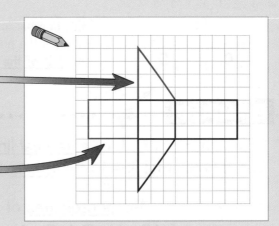

Those sneaky 3D shapes have always got a plan...

You can't see all of the faces of a 3D shape at once — some of them will be at the back or on the bottom of the shape. Don't forget them when you're drawing a net.

Coordinates

Go Across then Up to Find the Position

Each point on a grid has <u>two</u> numbers to show
its position. These are called <u>coordinates</u>.
Coordinates are always put in <u>brackets</u> like this: (1, 4).

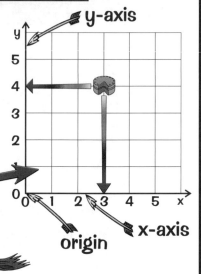

> Coordinates tell you how many <u>across</u> and how
> many <u>up or down</u> from the <u>origin</u> (0, 0) a point is.

EXAMPLE:

The cake's coordinates are: **(3, 4)**

The x-coordinate tells
you how many <u>across</u>.

The y-coordinate tells
you how many <u>up</u>.

The x-coordinate
always comes <u>before</u>
the y-coordinate.

Grids are Split into Four Quadrants

Each <u>quarter</u> of this diagram is called a <u>quadrant</u> — there are 4 quadrants.

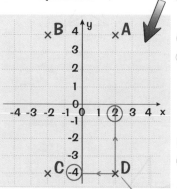

If this number is <u>positive</u>
it means the point is to
the <u>right of the origin</u>.

If this number is <u>positive</u>
it means the point is
<u>above the origin</u>.

(x, y)

If this number is <u>negative</u>
it means the point is to
the <u>left of the origin</u>.

If this number is <u>negative</u>
it means the point is
<u>below the origin</u>.

EXAMPLES:

From your point, draw a <u>vertical line</u> to the <u>x-axis</u> to find the <u>x-coordinate</u>
and a <u>horizontal line</u> to the <u>y-axis</u> to find the <u>y-coordinate</u>.

The <u>coordinates</u> of the points above are:
A (2, 4) B (–2, 4) C (–2, –4) D (2, –4)

"I can use coordinates in four quadrants."

Worked Examples

1 What are the coordinates of **point P**?

(5, 7)

1) Draw a <u>vertical line</u> from <u>point P</u> to the <u>x-axis</u>. It meets the x-axis at <u>5</u>.

2) Draw a <u>horizontal line</u> from <u>point P</u> to the <u>y-axis</u>. It meets the y-axis at <u>7</u>.

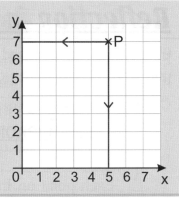

2 Plot the points **A (2, 3), B (–3, 1), C (–2, –2)** and **D (3, –2)** on the grid below.

1) To plot <u>point A</u>, read along the <u>x-axis</u> <u>+2 units</u>. Then read <u>up the grid</u> to the point that is in line with <u>3 on the y-axis</u>. Place a <u>cross</u> on the grid here.

2) The x-coordinate of <u>point B</u> is <u>–3</u>, so read 3 units to the <u>left</u> of the origin. Then read <u>up the grid</u> to the point that is in line with <u>1 on the y-axis</u>. Place a <u>cross</u> here.

3) <u>Repeat</u> for the coordinates of points C and D.

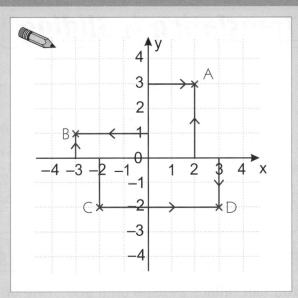

3 Find the **coordinates** of **point D** on this square.

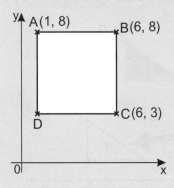

1) Point D has the <u>same</u> <u>x-coordinate</u> as point A.

2) Point D has the <u>same</u> <u>y-coordinate</u> as point C.

x-coordinate = 1

y-coordinate = 3

 The coordinates of point D are (1, 3).

I feel sorry for y — it always comes last...

Don't forget that the x-coordinate always comes first — it's really important.
A handy way to remember is that they're in alphabetical order — x first, then y.

Reflection and Translation

Reflection in a Line

Shapes can be reflected <u>in a line</u>. You call it the <u>mirror line</u> because the <u>image</u> you want is just what you'd see if you stuck a mirror on the paper along the line.

> B is the <u>image</u> of A reflected in the <u>MIRROR LINE</u>.

> Each point on the reflection B is the <u>SAME DISTANCE</u> from the mirror line as the same point on A.

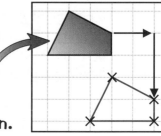

Mirror Line

Translation is Sliding

<u>Translation</u> is when a shape <u>slides</u> from one place to another, <u>without</u> rotating or flipping over.

EXAMPLE: Translate this shape 2 squares to the right and 3 squares down.

For <u>each corner</u>, go 2 squares to the right, 3 squares down and mark a cross. Then just <u>join up the crosses</u>.

Reflections and Translations on Grids

You can <u>reflect</u> a shape on a grid using one of the <u>axes</u> as a <u>mirror line</u>.
You can describe <u>translations</u> on grids using <u>numbers</u>.
A <u>positive number</u> means the shape moves <u>up or right</u>.
A <u>negative number</u> means the shape moves <u>down or left</u>.

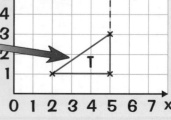

EXAMPLE:

<u>Translate</u> shape S <u>+2 units horizontally</u> and <u>−4 units vertically</u>.
Label the translated shape T.

> The shape slides <u>2 units right</u> and <u>4 units down</u>.

<u>ANSWER:</u>

For each point, count <u>2 units right</u> and <u>4 units down</u>, and draw the new point. Join the points up.

"I can reflect and translate shapes using coordinates."

Worked Examples

1 Translate shape M **5 squares to the left** and **3 squares up**.
Label the translated shape **N**.

1) For each corner, go <u>5 squares left</u> and
<u>3 squares up</u>. Mark a <u>cross</u> at each point.

2) <u>Join up</u> the crosses.

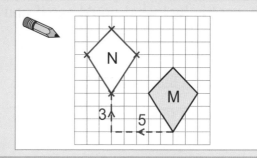

2 Shape Q is translated **−1 unit horizontally** and **−4 units vertically**.
Which **shape** is it translated onto?

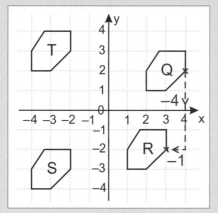

1) Pick a <u>point</u> on shape Q and <u>count 4 units down</u>
and <u>1 unit left</u> from it.

2) This is translated to the same point on <u>shape R</u>.

Shape R

3 **Reflect** shape A in the **x-axis**. Label this shape **B**.
Then **reflect** shape B in the **y-axis**. Label this shape **C**.

1) To reflect shape A, use the <u>x-axis</u> as a <u>mirror line</u>.

2) On shape A, look at how far each point is <u>above the</u>
<u>x-axis</u>. Mark each point the same distance <u>below the</u>
<u>x-axis</u> and join the points up.

3) To reflect shape B, use the <u>y-axis</u> as a <u>mirror line</u>.

4) On shape B, look at how far each point is to the <u>left</u>
of the <u>y-axis</u>. Mark each point the same distance
to the <u>right</u> of the <u>y-axis</u> and join the points up.

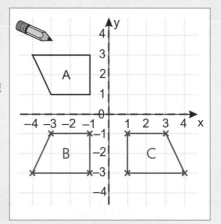

Sliding around on a grid — sounds like fun...

It's tempting to try to draw the translated or reflected shape all at once — but then
it's easier to make a mistake. Always translate or reflect each point separately.

Practice Questions

1 For each of these angles, say whether it is an acute, obtuse, reflex, or right angle.

    a)   123°   b)   17°

    c)   90°   d)   200°

2 Look at this diagram.

    Work out the size of angle x.

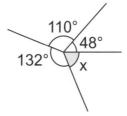

3 Find the missing angles a and b.

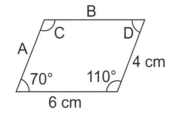

4 This shape is a parallelogram.

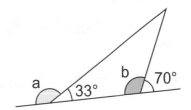

Work out the size of:

    a)   side A   b)   side B

    c)   angle C   d)   angle D

5 What type of triangle is this?

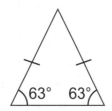

6 Which of these circles has a diameter of 5 cm?

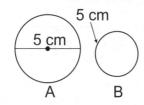

Not to scale

Practice Questions

7   Draw the plan view and the elevations of the front and the side of this cuboid.

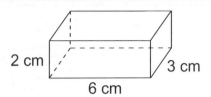

2 cm   3 cm
6 cm

8   Draw two different nets of a cube.

9   Four points are plotted on this grid.

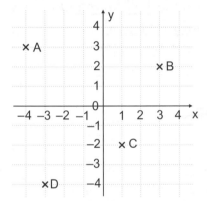

What are the coordinates of each point?

10   Shape X is shown on this set of axes.

a)   Reflect shape X in the y-axis.
Label this shape Y.

b)   Reflect shape Y in the x-axis.
Label this shape Z.

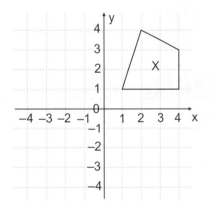

11   Shape A is shown on this set of axes.

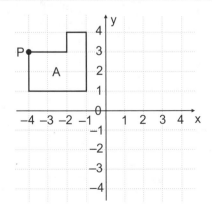

a)   Translate shape A +5 units horizontally
and −5 units vertically. Label this shape B.

b)   What are the coordinates of the
translated point P on shape B?

Tables

Data Can be Organised in a Table

Tables are a handy way of <u>organising</u> and <u>presenting</u> data neatly.

EXAMPLE:

Pirates Max, Ibrahim and Sue are digging for treasure.
They make a table showing how many
<u>gold</u> and <u>silver</u> coins they each find.

Use the information below to complete the table.

Pirate	Gold coins	Silver coins
Max	?	11
Ibrahim	24	?
Sue	28	16

Sue found <u>twenty eight gold</u> and <u>sixteen silver</u> coins.
Max found <u>eleven silver</u> coins and only <u>half as many</u> gold
coins as Sue. Ibrahim found <u>twenty four gold</u> coins and
as many <u>silver</u> coins as Max and Sue <u>put together</u>.

Max found <u>half as many</u> gold coins as Sue.
Sue found <u>28</u>, so Max found 28 ÷ 2 = <u>14</u>.

Pirate	Gold coins	Silver coins
Max	14	11
Ibrahim	24	27
Sue	28	16

Ibrahim found <u>as many</u> silver coins
as Max and Sue <u>put together</u>.

Max found <u>11</u> and Sue found <u>16</u>,
so Ibrahim found 11 + 16 = <u>27</u>.

Timetables Often Use the 24-Hour Clock

EXAMPLE:
Zwayne arrives at the <u>Rovus Space Shuttle Port</u> at 16:50.
What is the earliest time he can get to Astro?

1) Each column in the timetable gives you
the times for one space shuttle.

2) Find <u>Rovus</u> in the timetable and read along
that row until you find the first time after
16:50. It's <u>16:56</u>.

3) <u>Read down that column</u> to the 'Astro' row.
Hmm... that shuttle <u>doesn't stop</u> at Astro.
Try the next column — the 17:11 shuttle
<u>does</u> stop at Astro.

So Zwayne will get to Astro at <u>18:00</u>. ⌐ 18:00 is 6 pm. ¬

Rovus	16:41	16:56	17:11
Polon	16:55	17:10	17:25
Foxel	17:03	17:18	17:33
Wick	17:18	-	17:52
Astro	17:30	X	(18:00)
Barro	17:42	-	18:12

"I can complete, read and use information
in tables and timetables."

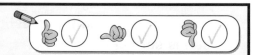

Worked Examples

1 The table below shows the lunch choices of each year group in a school. **50** Year 4 children had lunch. How many Year 4 children had **pizza**?

1) Find the Year 4 row.

2) The numbers in this row must add up to 50, so subtract to find the missing number.

Year	Pasta	Fish	Pizza
3	12	20	20
4	10	35	?
5	8	16	10
6	15	25	15

50 – 10 – 35 = 5
5 Year 4 children had pizza

2 The table shows the spelling test scores of three children. How many **more marks** did Bella get than Ken in **week 2**?

1) Find the week 2 row and read across until you get to Bella's and Ken's scores.

2) Subtract Ken's score from Bella's.

Week	Aidan	Bella	Ken
1	27	39	36
2	25	34	26

34 – 26 = 8
Bella got 8 more marks than Ken in week 2.

3 Barney needs to be in **Edstown** at **8.30 am**. What is the **latest time** he can catch the bus from **Morville**?

1) Find the Edstown row.

2) Read across it until you get to the last time before 8.30 am.

3) Read up that column until you get to the Morville row.

Alton	05:59	07:10	07:35
Morville	06:12	07:25	07:50
Carlton	06:32	07:45	08:10
Edstown	07:00	08:13	08:40
Tenton	07:18	08:35	09:00

Last time before 8.30 am   Too late

So the latest he can catch a bus from Morville is 7.25 am

Tables — good for organising data, and dinner...

With timetables, read the questions carefully. It's easy to mix up the time the person is setting off with the time they are getting to wherever they are going.

Bar Charts, Pictograms and Line Graphs

Line Graphs Show How Something Changes

EXAMPLE: Diana measured the height of rain water in a bucket <u>every two hours</u> one afternoon. She made a <u>line graph</u> of her results.
Estimate the change in height <u>between 2.00 pm and 5.00 pm</u>.

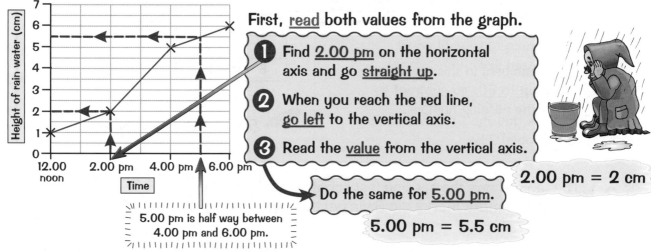

First, <u>read</u> both values from the graph.

1 Find <u>2.00 pm</u> on the horizontal axis and go <u>straight up</u>.

2 When you reach the red line, <u>go left</u> to the vertical axis.

3 Read the <u>value</u> from the vertical axis.

5.00 pm is half way between 4.00 pm and 6.00 pm.

Do the same for <u>5.00 pm</u>.

2.00 pm = 2 cm

5.00 pm = 5.5 cm

<u>Subtract</u> to find out the change in height <u>between 2.00 pm and 5.00 pm</u>.

5.5 cm – 2 cm = 3.5 cm

So the change in height between 2.00 pm and 5.00 pm was <u>3.5 cm</u>.

Pictograms use Pictures to show Data

EXAMPLE: This pictogram shows <u>how many tents</u> there were at Bear Woods Campsite each night one weekend.
How many <u>more</u> tents were there on <u>Saturday</u> than on <u>Sunday</u>?

This means <u>1 tent</u>. It's <u>half of 2</u>.

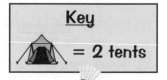

Key

= 2 tents

The <u>key</u> tells you what the pictures mean.

1) Find out how many <u>more pictures</u> there are next to <u>Saturday than Sunday</u>.

There are <u>4½ more pictures</u>.

2) Each picture means <u>2 tents</u>, and each ½ picture means <u>1 tent</u>. So there were:

(4 × 2) + 1 = <u>9 more tents</u> on Saturday than Sunday.

Bar charts work like pictograms but they have bars instead of pictures. You'll see one on the next page.

"I can solve problems using data from line graphs, pictograms and bar charts."

Worked Examples

1 The graph below shows the **weight** of a baby over 8 months.
How **old** was the baby when he reached **7 kg**?

1) Find <u>7 kg</u> on the <u>weight axis</u>.

2) Draw a line <u>across</u> until you meet the red line.

3) Then go <u>down</u> to the 'Age' axis. This gives you the <u>age</u> when the baby reached 7 kg.

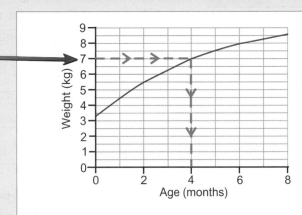

The baby reached 7 kg when he was

 4 months old.

2 The bar chart shows the number of each type of smoothie sold in a cafe one day. How many of the **two most popular** smoothies were sold **in total**?

1) The <u>height</u> of each bar tells you <u>how many</u> of that smoothie were sold.

2) Find the two <u>most popular</u> smoothies. These are the two with the <u>tallest bars</u> — <u>Melon Madness</u> and <u>Raspberry Rush</u>.

3) Read <u>across</u> from the top of these bars to find out <u>how many</u> of each were sold.

4) <u>Add</u> the numbers up to find the <u>total number</u> of these two smoothies sold.

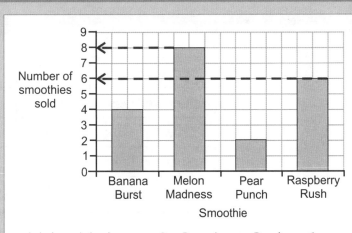

Melon Madness = 8, Raspberry Rush = 6
8 + 6 = 14

 14 of the two most popular smoothies were sold.

Baa, baa, bar chart...

Now and then you get a sideways bar chart, with bars that go across instead of up. Don't be put off. They work the same way — just read down to get the numbers.

Practice Questions

1   Oliver, Ryan and Katie went on a minibeast hunt.
The table below shows the number of minibeasts Ryan and Oliver caught.

	Oliver	Ryan	Katie
Spider	12	26	
Ant	16	12	
Earwig	3	15	

a)   Katie caught **three fewer** spiders than Ryan and the **same number** of ants as him. She caught **four times as many** earwigs as Oliver.
Use this information to complete the table.

b)   How many earwigs were caught in total?

c)   How many more minibeasts did Ryan catch in total that Oliver?

2   Here is the timetable for a steam train.

Owl Moor	10:40	12:00	14:15
Vulture Pass	10:55	12:15	14:30
Crow Crossing	11:18	12:38	14:53
Sparrow Town	11:48	-	15:23
Rook's End	12:02	-	15:37

a)   How long does the train take to get from Owl Moor to Crow Crossing?

b)   Mary hikes to Vulture Pass station. She gets there at 13:00 and gets on the next train. What time does she get to Rook's End?

c)   Brian is meeting a friend at Sparrow Town station at 12 noon.
What time should he get the train from Crow Crossing?

Practice Questions

3   Jasmine records the temperature in her garden every hour.
She draws a line graph of her results.

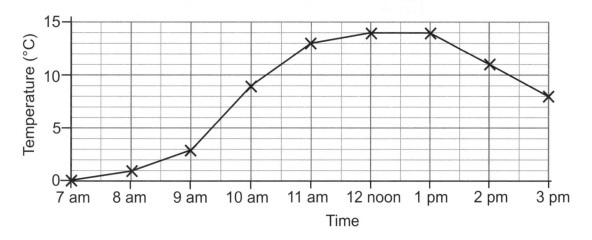

a)   What was the highest temperature recorded by Jasmine?

b)   Jasmine took her coat off at 11 am.
What was the temperature when she took her coat off?

c)   How much did the temperature fall by between 1 pm and 3 pm?

4   Rupert records the eye colours of all the children in Class 5 and Class 6.
He makes a bar chart for Class 5's results and a pictogram for Class 6's.

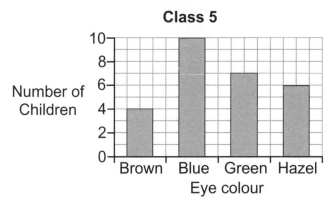
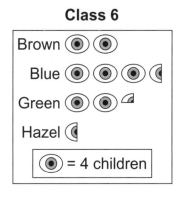

a)   How many children are there in **Class 5**?

b)   How many children in **Class 6** have **blue** eyes?

c)   How many **more** children in Class 6 than in Class 5
have **brown** eyes?

Answers

Pages 12-13 — Section One

1) a) **Six hundred**
   b) **Three million, eight hundred and seventy two thousand, six hundred and fifty one**
2) **£600 281**
3) **6 812 993, 6 782 149, 696 999, 582 107**
   Descending order means from biggest to smallest.
4) 3425 is bigger than 3347, so **Angelina** has the most songs.
5) a) Floor **–4**
   b) Floor **–6**
6) There are 6 places from –6 to 0,
   then 5 places from 0 to 5.
   So 6 + 5 = **11 °C**
7) **–7 + 8 = 1, so Colin is not correct.**
   Don't forget to show why he isn't correct
   — you can't just say 'he's not correct'.
8) a) **1066**
   c) MMIII = 2003
   Roswell was founded in 2003, which is after 1066, so it was founded **after** Buckhead.
9) a) **Six hundredths**
   b) **Two thousandths**
10) **8.104, 8.32, 8.4, 12.25, 12.3**
    The first thing to do when ordering decimals is to line all the numbers up and give all them the same number of decimal places by adding in zeros.
11) 68.35 is bigger than 68.306,
    so **Lee** cycled the furthest.
12) a) **8 523 400**
    b) **8 520 000**
    c) **9 000 000**
13) **2 kg**
14) **7.2 m**

Pages 32-33 — Section Two

1) a)
$$
\begin{array}{r}
8\ 4\ 7\ 5 \\
+\ \ 4\ 1\ 2\ 3 \\
\hline
1\ 2\ 5\ 9\ 8 \\
\end{array}
$$

b)
$$
\begin{array}{r}
5\ 1\ 4\ 3\ 2 \\
+\ \ \ \ 7\ 3\ 8\ 4 \\
\hline
5\ 8\ 8\ 1\ 6 \\
\end{array}
$$

c)
$$
\begin{array}{r}
6\ 8\ 7\ 5\ 4 \\
-\ \ \ \ 4\ 9\ 8\ 2 \\
\hline
6\ 3\ 7\ 7\ 2 \\
\end{array}
$$

2)
$$
\begin{array}{r}
6\ 5\ .\ 8\ 4 \\
+\ \ \ 4\ .\ 2\ 3 \\
1\ 8\ .\ 4\ 9 \\
\hline
8\ 8\ .\ 5\ 6 \\
\end{array}
$$
So Rachel spends **£88.56** in total.

3)
$$
\begin{array}{r}
2\ 7\ 4\ .\ 9\ 3 \\
-\ \ \ \ \ 7\ .\ 8\ 5 \\
\hline
2\ 6\ 7\ .\ 0\ 8 \\
\end{array}
$$
Emily can run 800 m in **267.08 seconds**.
This is just a subtraction question in disguise. Don't be put off by all the words in the question — the maths is just the same.

4) a)
$$
\begin{array}{r}
6\ 1\ 4 \\
\times\ \ \ \ 2\ 3 \\
\hline
1\ 8\ 4\ 2 \\
1\ 2\ 2\ 8\ 0 \\
\hline
1\ 4\ 1\ 2\ 2 \\
\end{array}
$$

b)
$$
\begin{array}{r}
2\ 8\ 7\ 3 \\
\times\ \ \ \ \ \ 1\ 5 \\
\hline
1\ 4\ 3\ 6\ 5 \\
2\ 8\ 7\ 3\ 0 \\
\hline
4\ 3\ 0\ 9\ 5 \\
\end{array}
$$

Answers

5)
$$
\begin{array}{r}
4\ 3\ 0\ 2 \\
\times\qquad 7 \\
\hline
3\ 0\ 1\ 1\ 4 \\
{}_2\ {}_1
\end{array}
= \textbf{30 114 g}
$$

6)
$$
12\,\overline{)\,1\ {}^{1}3\ {}^{1}6\ {}^{4}8\,}\quad \begin{array}{c} 1\ 1\ 4 \end{array} = \textbf{114 cable cars}
$$

7)   a)
$$
7\,\overline{)\,2\ {}^{2}6\ {}^{5}4\ {}^{5}5\,}\quad\begin{array}{c}3\ 7\ 7\end{array}\,\text{r}\,6 = \textbf{377 r 6}
$$

b) $\mathbf{377\dfrac{6}{7}}$

When you write your answer as a mixed number, the remainder is the top number of the fraction and the number you're dividing by is the bottom number.

8)   a) $\mathbf{35} \times 100 = 3500$
b) $0.24 \times 10 = \textbf{2.4}$
c) $6.74 \times \mathbf{1000} = 6740$
d) $\mathbf{59.82} \times 1000 = 59\ 820$

9) $6724 \div 100 = \textbf{67.24 km}$

10)   a) $16 - 4 \times 2 + 3 = 16 - 8 + 3 = \mathbf{11}$
b) $8 \times (6 - 1) + 12 = 8 \times 5 + 12 = 40 + 12 = \mathbf{52}$
Remember the BODMAS rules for these questions.

11) $\mathbf{(12 + 6) \div 3}$

12)   a)   E.g. $6 \times 8 = \mathbf{48}$
b)   E.g. $200 \div (4 \times 5) = 200 \div 20 = \mathbf{10}$
You might end up with different answers if you round to different numbers — but always make sure you round to a sensible number.

13)   a) $\mathbf{4, 8, 12, 16, 20}$
b) $\mathbf{12, 24, 36, 48, 60}$

14)   a)   Factors of 30: **1 and 30, 2 and 15, 3 and 10, 5 and 6**
b)   Factors of 49: **1 and 49, 7**

15)   a) $\mathbf{19, 23}$
b) $\mathbf{59, 61, 67}$

16) $18 = \mathbf{2 \times 3 \times 3}$

17) $3^2 = 3 \times 3 = 9$
$2^3 = 2 \times 2 \times 2 = 8$
$9 + 8 = 17$
So Gunther is thinking of **9** and **8**.

Pages 48-49 — Section Three

1)   a)   There are $3 \times 7 = 21$ sevenths in 3, so there are $21 + 3 = 24$ sevenths in total.
So $3\dfrac{3}{7} = \dfrac{\mathbf{24}}{\mathbf{7}}$

b) $14 \div 5 = 2$ remainder 4, so $\dfrac{14}{5} = \mathbf{2\dfrac{4}{5}}$

2)   Total number of pieces eaten $= 6 + 9 + 8 = 23$.
The denominator will be 10, so they have eaten $\dfrac{23}{10}$ bars.
$23 \div 10 = 2$ remainder 3, so $\dfrac{23}{10} = 2\dfrac{3}{10}$.
They have eaten $\mathbf{2\dfrac{3}{10}}$ chocolate bars.

3) $\dfrac{5}{6} = \dfrac{\mathbf{10}}{\mathbf{12}}$

4)   2, 9 and 6 all have 18 as a multiple, so use that as a common denominator:
$\dfrac{1}{2} = \dfrac{9}{18},\ \dfrac{4}{9} = \dfrac{8}{18},\ \dfrac{5}{6} = \dfrac{15}{18}$
In order from largest to smallest: $\dfrac{15}{18},\ \dfrac{9}{18},\ \dfrac{8}{18}$
So the order is: $\dfrac{\mathbf{5}}{\mathbf{6}},\ \dfrac{\mathbf{1}}{\mathbf{2}},\ \dfrac{\mathbf{4}}{\mathbf{9}}$

5)   a) $21 \div 3 = 7$
$7 \times 2 = 14$
So $\dfrac{2}{3} \times 21 = \mathbf{14}$

b) $2 \times 25 = 50$
$25 \div 5 = 5,\ 5 \times 3 = 15$
$50 + 15 = 65$
So $2\dfrac{3}{5} \times 25 = \mathbf{65}$

6)   a) $\dfrac{1}{3} \times \dfrac{1}{4} = \dfrac{1 \times 1}{3 \times 4} = \dfrac{\mathbf{1}}{\mathbf{12}}$

b) $\dfrac{3}{8} \times \dfrac{7}{10} = \dfrac{3 \times 7}{8 \times 10} = \dfrac{\mathbf{21}}{\mathbf{80}}$

7)   a) $\dfrac{8}{15} + \dfrac{11}{15} + \dfrac{4}{15} = \dfrac{8 + 11 + 4}{15} = \dfrac{23}{15} = \mathbf{1\dfrac{8}{15}}$

b)   There are 10 tenths in a whole, so there are $10 + 9 = 19$ tenths in $1\dfrac{9}{10}$.
$1\dfrac{9}{10} + \dfrac{3}{10} - \dfrac{1}{10} = \dfrac{19 + 3 - 1}{10} = \dfrac{21}{10} = \mathbf{2\dfrac{1}{10}}$

Answers

8) a) 8 and 12 both have 24 as a multiple,
so use that as the common denominator.
$\frac{7}{8} = \frac{21}{24}$ and $\frac{5}{12} = \frac{10}{24}$
So $\frac{7}{8} - \frac{5}{12} = \frac{21}{24} - \frac{10}{24} = \frac{21-10}{24} = \frac{11}{24}$

b) 3 and 7 both have 21 as a multiple,
so use that as the common denominator.
$\frac{1}{3} = \frac{7}{21}$ and $\frac{2}{7} = \frac{6}{21}$
So $\frac{1}{3} + \frac{2}{7} = \frac{7}{21} + \frac{6}{21} = \frac{7+6}{21} = \frac{13}{21}$

9) The calculation you need to do is $\frac{4}{5} - \frac{1}{4}$
5 and 4 both have 20 as a multiple,
so use that as the common denominator.
$\frac{4}{5} = \frac{16}{20}$ and $\frac{1}{4} = \frac{5}{20}$
So $\frac{4}{5} - \frac{1}{4} = \frac{16}{20} - \frac{5}{20} = \frac{16-5}{20} = \frac{11}{20}$

10) a) $\frac{1}{8} \div 4 = \frac{1}{8 \times 4} = \frac{1}{32}$

b) $\frac{2}{5} \div 7 = \frac{2}{5 \times 7} = \frac{2}{35}$

11) The calculation you need to do is $\frac{1}{5} \div 3$:
$\frac{1}{5} \div 3 = \frac{1}{5 \times 3} = \frac{1}{15}$

12) a) $0.219 = \frac{219}{1000}$

b) $0.49 = \frac{49}{100}$

c) $\frac{16}{25} = \frac{64}{100} = 0.64$

d) $\frac{3}{500} = \frac{6}{1000} = 0.06$

13) a) $0.39 \times 100 = 39\%$
b) $13 \div 100 = 0.13$

14) $\frac{11}{50} = \frac{22}{100} = 22\%$ of his T-shirts are white.

15) $100\% - 60\% = 40\%$ of Scott's friends
are not at his birthday party. $40\% = 0.4 = \frac{2}{5}$

Pages 60-61 — Section Four

1) £56 ÷ 8 = **£7**
2) 6 bought tickets : 1 free ticket
30 bought tickets = 5 × 6 bought tickets
So she gets 5 × 1 = **5 free tickets**
3) 15 people = 3 × 5 people
So he needs: 3 × 15 = **45 sandwiches**
and 3 × 10 = **30 sausage rolls**
4) Number of shares = 6 + 5 = 11
One share = 66 ÷ 11 = £6
Monisha gets 6 × 6 = **£36**
Vicky gets 5 × 6 = **£30**
5) a) Rahul's items : Sarah's items = **2 : 3**
b) 18 = 2 × 9, so Sarah sold 3 × 9 = **27 items**
6) a) £160 ÷ 10 = **£16**
b) 10% of 120 kg = 120 ÷ 10 = 12 kg
5% of 120 kg = 12 ÷ 2 = 6 kg
15% of 120kg = 12 + 6 = **18 kg**
c) 70 cm ÷ 10 = 7 cm
7 cm × 3 = **21 cm**
7) The club has 18 + 7 = 25 members.
$\frac{7}{25} = \frac{7 \times 4}{25 \times 4} = \frac{28}{100}$
28%
8) She got 20 − 4 = 16 questions right.
$\frac{16}{20} = \frac{16 \times 5}{20 \times 5} = \frac{80}{100}$
80%
9) $6 \times 8 \times \frac{1}{2} = 48 \times \frac{1}{2} = \textbf{24 cm}^2$
10) **Number of bananas = 6 × number of apples**
11) **Total booking fee = £15 × number of people**
12) a) ☆ = 104 − 7 = **97**   b) ☐ = 37 + 15 = **52**
c) ○ = 96 ÷ 8 = **12**   d) △ = 7 × 12 = **84**
13) R = Ryan's money
£48 = 8 × R
R = £48 ÷ 8 = **£6**
14) E.g.
If **M = 1**: 3M = 3, so 3 + N = 17 and **N = 14**
If **M = 2**: 3M = 6, so 6 + N = 17 and **N = 11**
If **M = 3**: 3M = 9, so 9 + N = 17 and **N = 8**
If **M = 4**: 3M = 12, so 12 + N = 17 and **N = 5**

Answers

Pages 74-75 — Section Five

1) a) 3 × 16 = **48 ounces**
   b) 64 ÷ 16 = **4 lbs**
2) a) 5 cm × 3 = 15 cm, so 2 inches × 3 = **6 inches**
   b) 2 inches × 10 = 20 inches,
   so 5 cm × 10 = **50 cm**
3) 24 × 3 = 72, so 84 ÷ 24 = 3 r 12
   So it takes her **3 days and 12 hours**.
4) 3 litres = 3 × 1000 = 3000 ml
   3000 ÷ 500 = **6 bottles**
5) £3.85 = 3.85 × 100 = 385p
   385p + 79p = 464p
   464 ÷ 100 = **£4.64**
   You could also work out the answer to this question
   by converting 79p into pounds (£0.79), and then
   adding that to £3.85.
6) 1.37 m = 1.37 × 100 = 137 cm
   42 mm = 42 ÷ 10 = 4.2 cm
   137 + 4.2 = **141.2 cm**
7) 20 + 8 + (20 − 16 − 2) + 9 +
   16 + 9 + 2 + 8 = **74 cm**
   Use the lengths of the opposite sides to find the
   missing sides.
8) 18 ÷ 6 = **3 m**
9) **11.5 m²**
10) a) 9 × 9 = **81 cm²**
    b) 7 × 6 = **42 m²**
    c) $\frac{1}{2}$ × 3 × 8 = **12 mm²**
    d) 4 × 9 = **36 cm²**
11) Area of parallelogram: 10 × 8 = 80 mm²
    Area of one triangle: $\frac{1}{2}$ × 5 × 8 = 20 mm²
    Total area: 80 + 20 + 20 = **120 mm²**
12) 3 × 4 × 6 = **72 cm³**
13) 5 × 2 × height = 100
    height = 100 ÷ 10 = **10 cm**

Pages 86-87 — Section Six

1) a) **Obtuse**   c) **Right angle**
   b) **Acute**   d) **Reflex**
2) x = 360° − 132° − 110° − 48° = **70°**
3) a = 180° − 33° = **147°**
   b = 180° − 70° = **110°**
4) a) **4 cm**   c) **110°**
   b) **6 cm**   d) **70°**
5) The triangle has two equal length sides and two
   equal angles. **It is an isosceles triangle**.
6) **Circle A**
7) Plan: Elevation:

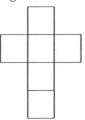

8) E.g.

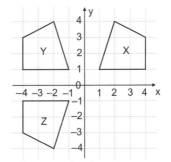

9) A (−4, 3)   B (3, 2)
   C (1, −2)   D (−3, −4)
10)

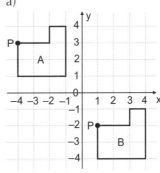

11) a)

b) **(1, −2)**

Answers

Pages 92-93 — Section Seven

1) a)

	Oliver	Ryan	Katie
Spider	12	26	26 − 3 = **26**
Ant	16	12	**12**
Earwig	3	15	3 × 4 = **12**

   b) 3 + 15 + 12 = **30**

   c) Ryan caught 26 + 12 + 15 = 53 minibeasts.
       Oliver caught 12 + 16 + 3 = 31 minibeasts.
       So Ryan caught 53 − 31 = **22 more than Oliver**.

2) a) This is easiest to work out using the second train. It leaves Owl Moor at 12:00 and arrives at Crow Crossing at 12:38.
       So the journey takes **38 minutes**.

   b) The next train from Vulture Pass is at 14:30.
       It gets to Rook's End at **15:37**.

   c) The first train is the only one to get to Sparrow Town before noon. Brian must get the train from Crow Crossing at **11:18**.

3) a) **14 °C**

   b) Go up from 11 am on the time axis until you get to the line. Then go across until you reach the other axis. This gives you the temperature at 11 am, which was **13 °C**.

   c) Go up from 1 pm on the time axis until you reach the line. Then go across until you reach the other axis and read off the temperature at that point. Repeat for 3 pm.
       At 1 pm it was 14 °C. At 3 pm it was 8 °C.
       So it fell 14 − 8 = **6 °C**

4) a) To find the number of children in Class 5, add up the heights of all the bars.
       4 + 10 + 7 + 6 = **27**

   b) There are 3½ pictures next to 'Blue'.
       Each picture means 4 children, so each ½ picture means 4 ÷ 2 = 2 children.
       So there are (3 × 4) + 2 = 12 + 2 = **14 children with blue eyes**.

   c) Reading from the bar chart, 4 children in Class 5 have brown eyes.
       There are 2 pictures next to 'Brown' in the pictogram, so 2 × 4 = 8 children in Class 6 have brown eyes.
       So 8 − 4 = **4 more children** in Class 6 than in Class 5 have brown eyes.

Index

Index

MJ ER21